TEENS IN ISRAEL

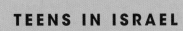

Teens in

Israel

BY Michael Burgan

Content Adviser: Karen Grumberg, Ph.D.,
Department of Middle Eastern Studies,
University of Texas at Austin

Reading Adviser: Katie Van Sluys, Ph.D.,
Department of Teacher Education,
DePaul University

Compass Point Books Minneapolis, Minnesota

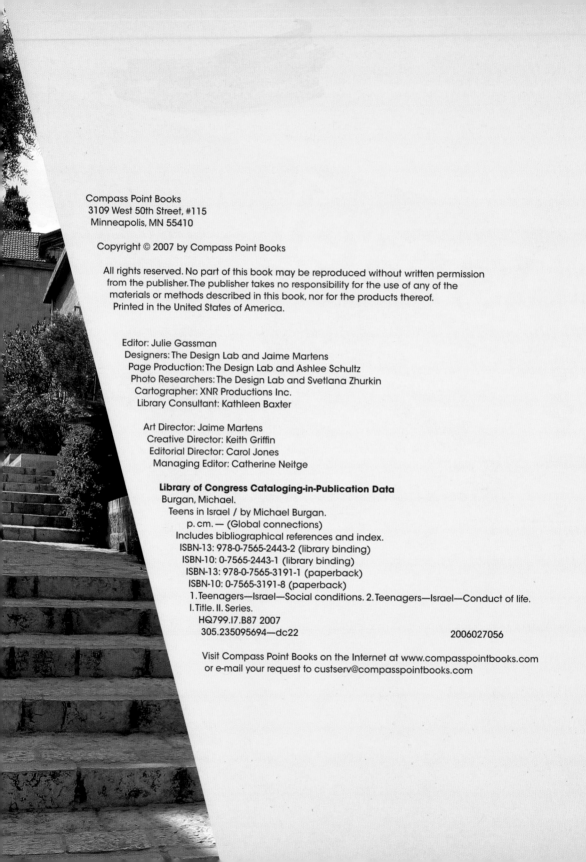

Compass Point Books
3109 West 50th Street, #115
Minneapolis, MN 55410

Editor: Julie Gassman
Designers: The Design Lab and Jaime Martens
Page Production: The Design Lab and Ashlee Schultz
Photo Researchers: The Design Lab and Svetlana Zhurkin
Cartographer: XNR Productions Inc.
Library Consultant: Kathleen Baxter

Art Director: Jaime Martens
Creative Director: Keith Griffin
Editorial Director: Carol Jones
Managing Editor: Catherine Neitge

Library of Congress Cataloging-in-Publication Data
Burgan, Michael.
  Teens in Israel / by Michael Burgan.
    p. cm. — (Global connections)
  Includes bibliographical references and index.
    ISBN-13: 978-0-7565-2443-2 (library binding)
    ISBN-10: 0-7565-2443-1 (library binding)
    ISBN-13: 978-0-7565-3191-1 (paperback)
    ISBN-10: 0-7565-3191-8 (paperback)
    1. Teenagers—Israel—Social conditions. 2. Teenagers—Israel—Conduct of life.
  I. Title. II. Series.
    HQ799.I7.B87 2007
    305.235095694—dc22   2006027056

Visit Compass Point Books on the Internet at www.compasspointbooks.com
or e-mail your request to custserv@compasspointbooks.com

Table of Contents

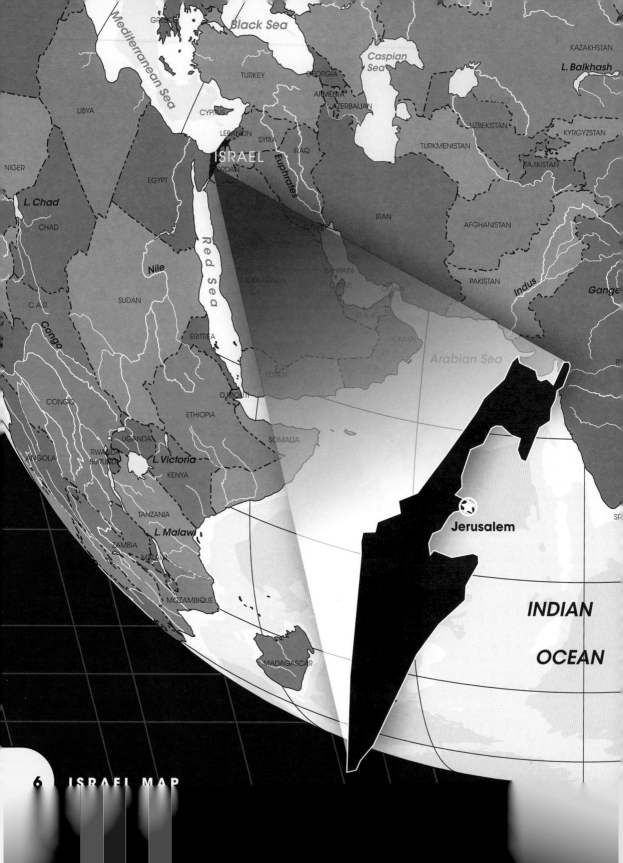

GREECE

Black Sea

Caspian Sea

KAZAKHSTAN

L. Balkhash

Mediterranean Sea

TURKEY

GEORGIA

ARMENIA

AZERBAIJAN

UZBEKISTAN

KYRGYZSTAN

LIBYA

CYPRUS

LEBANON

SYRIA

IRAQ

TURKMENISTAN

TAJIKISTAN

NIGER

ISRAEL

JORDAN

Euphrates

IRAN

AFGHANISTAN

EGYPT

Nile

SAUDI ARABIA

BAHRAIN

QATAR

OMAN

PAKISTAN

Indus

Ganges

L. Chad

CHAD

U.A.E.

C.A.R.

SUDAN

Red Sea

OMAN

Arabian Sea

IN

Congo

ERITREA

YEMEN

DJIBOUTI

ETHIOPIA

CONGO

SOMALIA

ANGOLA

UGANDA

RWANDA
BURUNDI

L. Victoria

KENYA

Jerusalem

SR

TANZANIA

L. Malawi

ZAMBIA

MALAWI

INDIAN

MOZAMBIQUE

OCEAN

MADAGASCAR

MONGOLIA

Huang

CHINA

Yangtze

NORTH KOREA

SOUTH KOREA

Yellow
Sea

East
China
Sea

BHUTAN

NEPAL

BANGLADESH

MYANMAR

Salween

VIETNAM

LAOS

Mekong

THAILAND

KAMPUCHEA

PHILIPPINES

South
China
Sea

Bay
of
Bengal

BRUNEI

MALAYSIA

MALAYSIA

SINGAPORE

INDONESIA

THERE ARE MORE THAN 2.1 MILLION YOUNG PEOPLE UNDER THE AGE OF 18 IN ISRAEL. They live in a modern nation, heavily influenced by Europe and the United States. Skyscrapers, the Internet, and cell phones are all part of daily life. Yet they know that Israel is a land where Jews have lived for thousands of years.

It is also a land that is often filled with conflict between Israelis and Palestinians, an Arab people who also claim the area as their homeland. This struggle has led to several wars and created problems for Arabs who are citizens of Israel. They often find themselves under suspicion, as Israeli Jews question their loyalty to the country.

Tensions between Israelis and Palestinians are ongoing, and sometimes violence erupts. Israeli teens live in a country laced with tight security. The threat of a bombing or an enemy attack is always present. But the young people do not live in fear. They believe in their right to live on this land. And they take pleasure in friends, family, good food, travel, and leisure.

9

All students, including new immigrants, are required to learn to read and write Hebrew.

1

Different Cultures, Different Schools

TWO TEACHERS STAND AT THE FRONT OF THE CLASSROOM AT THE SCHOOL IN NEVE SHALOM–WAHAT AL-SALAM, ISRAEL. The community's dual name is the Hebrew and Arabic phrases for "Oasis of Peace." The teachers reflect these two cultures as well. One is a Jewish Israeli who teaches in Hebrew. The other is an Arab Israeli who teaches in Arabic. The students in Neve Shalom–Wahat al-Salam come from both Jewish and Arab families, and they'll be taught in the two official languages of Israel through sixth grade. Their school and their town, where Arabs and Jews live side by side, are part of a plan to bridge the gap that separates the two main cultures in Israel.

Such an effort to bring together Arab and Jewish children, however, is rare in Israel. The students of Neve Shalom–Wahat al-Salam will most likely go to high schools that teach only Jewish or Arab students, though there are hopes of building a high school in Jerusalem for both cultures.

From the outside, Israel might seem like a united land—a country founded by Jews in 1948 to re-create the former Jewish state of Israel, an ancient kingdom with roots dating back to around 2000 B.C. But the country's schools show the wide diversity that exists in a country where 20 percent of the more than 6.3 million people are Arab.

Many Types of Schools

Schooling starts at age 5, and by law children must stay in school until they are 15. In elementary school, kids go to schools in their neighborhoods. High school, which begins in ninth grade, may be farther from home, so students get rides from their parents or take public transportation, such as buses or trains. Walking or biking is common, too, and some private-school students live at their schools.

Israel has several types of schools, from religious to secular to Arab. What students learn depends on the kind of school they attend and their family background. One thing, however, is constant in all Jewish schools, including the secular: Students study the Tanahk, the Hebrew bible.

The Ashkenazim, Jews who originally came from Europe, tend to have better-paying jobs than other Israelis. As a result their communities often have secular high schools that prepare students for college. They offer courses in math, science, literature, language, and history. Individual schools might also have a particular focus, such as science, the arts, or military training.

In secular schools, students can often choose from a wide range of electives.

Types of Israeli Schools

State Schools
Secular Jewish
Religious Jewish
Arab—including separate schools for Druze (members of an isolated religion and community)

Private Schools
Religious
Secular
Foreign Language—including Russian and English

How Israel Came to Be

Jewish settlers, many from Europe, created the modern nation of Israel in 1948. They sought to reclaim the land where their ancestors lived more than 3,000 years ago, and where some Jews still lived at the time of Israel's rebirth. Most Jews had long ago spread around the world in a movement called the Diaspora. The lands where they settled were also given that name.

During the 19th century, some European Jews supported Zionism, the belief that Jews were entitled to have their own nation in the traditional lands of Israel. In the 1880s, Zionists began immigrating to what was then Palestine.

For Jews, the process of leaving one's country to go to Israel is called *aliyah*, or "going up." The European Jews of the first aliyah were mostly secular. Being Jewish was part of their culture, but they did not follow all the laws of the Torah, the Jewish religious text. The Jews who returned to Israel brought with them the foods and cultures of the lands where they had settled.

In the 1930s a number of factories were built by recent arrivals to Israel. This effort helped build an economy.

aliyah
ali-YAH

The Jews of the new Israel not only had various homelands. They also had various views on religion. While the founders of Israel were secular, other Jews in the new Israel practiced a strict brand of Judaism. They closely followed the teachings in the Torah. Today Jewish religious law influences how all Israelis marry and divorce, when shops close, and how people eat. Secular Israeli Jews—and non-Jewish Israelis—sometimes feel unfairly limited by these laws.

Teen Scenes

Hopping on a minibus, a 14-year-old boy crosses the streets of Haifa, the third-largest city in Israel, as he heads to another day of school. He and about 30 other Jewish students will crowd into their classrooms, where they're taught in Hebrew. He learns English as well, and outside the classroom, the teen hears Russian and other languages, because many of his classmates are immigrants. Computer science is his favorite course, and he hopes to work with computers when he enters the army. Because Israel faces an almost constant threat of terrorism, nearly all secular Jewish teens are required to serve in the military after they finish school.

About 95 miles (158 kilometer) away, in the ancient city of Jerusalem, a young ultra-Orthodox teen walks to his neighborhood religious school. Most of his class time is devoted to studying the Torah. His sister, like other ultra-Orthodox girls, goes to a separate school, where she combines courses such as science, math, and English with her religious work. Unlike secular teens, the brother and sister will not have to serve in the military after high school. The boy most likely will continue his religious studies, while his sister will marry, start a family, and look for a job to support her children and husband, who will likely be a religious scholar like her brother.

In another part of Jerusalem, an Arab Israeli also walks to class. His high school is a crumbling building, and the books are old. He and his classmates are more likely than Jewish teens to drop out of school, and much less likely to go to college. He won't be allowed to serve in the military, so he will likely miss out on friendships that help many Israelis find high paying jobs. The Arab teen will have to work hard to escape the poverty and prejudice that many Israeli Arabs face.

Israel is a small land with a huge variety of people, where Jewish culture and religion shape the country's laws. For teens, their families' faith and ethnic backgrounds play a large role in determining the kind of education they receive and what they will do as adults.

At the Neveh Channah girls' school, teachings on Jewish marriage and family are included.

The Languages of Israel

Immigrants from countries that did not have democracy take special courses to learn about the political system and their responsibilities in a democracy.

Jews from North Africa and the Middle East are called Mizrahim. Many of them live in poorer communities. Their high schools focus more on preparing students for jobs, rather than for college. These vocational schools teach practical skills such as electronics or bookkeeping. In recent years, some Mizrahim have started special programs to prepare their students for the *bagruts*, the exams students must pass to enter college. Orthodox and *haredi,* or ultra-Orthodox, students make up about 35 percent of Israel's high

bagrut
bah-GROOT

haredi
hare-DEE

Fewer than two dozen Israeli elementary schools teach Arabic to Jewish students. Starting in seventh grade, Jewish students are supposed to study Arabic for four years. In reality, however, only about half do. Not all schools can afford to teach it, and many students are not interested in learning it. Only 3,000 Jewish high school students a year take Arabic through their last year of high school and then take the bagrut, or exam, for that course. Arab Israelis are required to take Hebrew starting in second grade. All Israeli students study English starting in third grade and continue through high school, making English a commonly used language in Israel.

The Yeshivot

Orthodox and haredi students pursue religious studies in a special school called a *yeshiva*. Yeshivot (the plural) are geared for various age groups, starting with studies in grade seven. Yeshiva students study the Torah and other religious teachings. After age 18, young men can go to yeshivot that train them to be rabbis or religious scholars. These students are not required to join the military, like other Jewish Israelis are. Their religious study is considered part of their service to the nation. Young haredi women, after they finish school, often marry young and start families. Some work outside the home to support their families, because their husbands continue their religious studies throughout their lives.

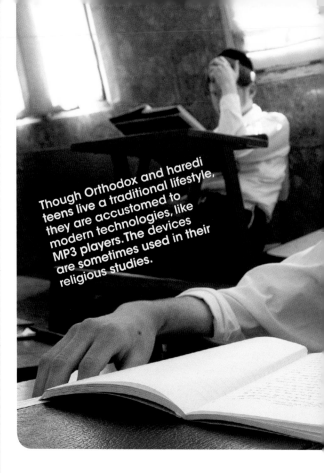

Though Orthodox and haredi teens live a traditional lifestyle, they are accustomed to modern technologies, like MP3 players. The devices are sometimes used in their religious studies.

yeshiva
yeh-shi-VAH

school students. Some Orthodox schools stress the need to accept the modern ways of life. Students at these schools take the same kinds of courses as the secular schools, with the addition of Jewish religious teachings.

The more conservative Orthodox and the haredim believe that following traditional Jewish customs and religion are the most important tasks in life. At school these students spend even more time on religious studies and less on academics. Haredi boys and girls attend separate schools, because most branches of ultra-Orthodox Judaism believe that

men and women should not be together in public.

Schools in Arab communities are often affected by poverty, which has been rising in Israel, especially among Arabs. The discrimination they face from Jews has limited their ability to gain political power or obtain good jobs. In 2004, 50 percent of all Arab Israeli families were considered poor, up from 48.4 percent the year before. The schools in these poorer communities tend to have fewer computers and other modern teaching tools than Jewish schools in wealthier areas. Arab students tend to drop out more frequently than Jewish students. Only about 5 percent of college graduates are Arab, although slightly more than 50 percent pass the exam that allows them to apply for college.

In the Classroom

The typical secular high school class might have as many as 40 students jammed into the room, with students routinely calling their teachers by their first names. One young teacher at a Tel Aviv high school said, "For them (Israeli students) school is like camp—there is no discipline or regulations." A 17-year-old student at the same school agreed. After spending two months at a U.S. school, she saw that the rules were much stricter there than at her school. In Israel, she said, "People don't invest in school for their future."

However, in recent years, schools have tried to bring some order to the

Schools for Arab students tend to have larger classes with high student to teacher ratios.

At the Democratic School in Hadera, students are allowed to decide if they want to go to class; pursue activities like music, sports, or art; or spend time talking and socializing.

classroom. More schools are requiring students to wear uniforms, and some students now address their teachers as "Teacher" or by their last names.

In 2005, the government lengthened the school day of the secular schools. Students now attend classes from 8 A.M. until 4 P.M., though the school week in some schools was shortened from six to five days. Jews do not attend school on Saturday, their Sabbath, while Muslims are off on Friday, the Islamic holy day.

At some Jewish schools, students spend Fridays on extracurricular activities instead of regular classes. The extracurricular activities vary widely. Students may play sports, belong to clubs, play instruments, and perform in plays.

Some other activities are linked to safety. The country faces an almost constant threat of attack from neighboring Arab countries. Palestinian terrorists are also a concern. In fifth grade, students take a five-day course that prepares them for emergencies, including how to use gas masks in case of a chemical attack. In addition, schools often have armed guards at the doors. To enter most public buildings, Israelis pass by guards, who search them and their bags for weapons.

The fear of violence, however, doesn't keep students from living their daily lives. Adam Argeband, 18, who moved from England to Israel, said, "You … are never deterred by terrorists to not go out, ever."

Young Israelis aren't afraid to attend school or go places with their friends. Meanwhile, the adults try to find solutions to the country's hardest problems. They hope the education their children—Jewish and Arab—receive will help make the process easier in the future.

The Conflict

Israel was created out of Palestine, land that the Palestinians called home. When the Jewish nation was established, the Palestinian people were angry. With the establishment of Israel, the Palestinians lost much of their homeland. In May 1948, Egypt, Jordan, and Syria, which supported the Palestinians, attacked Israel in an attempt to take back the land. The Israelis were able to defeat the Arab countries by January 1949. Thousands of Palestinians left the country, and those who stayed were often treated poorly and faced discrimination.

In the 1960s, the Palestine Liberation Organization (PLO) was formed to represent the Palestinians in their battle against Israel. In the years since, some PLO members have turned to violence in the form of terrorist attacks and intifadas, or uprisings, to oppose Jewish rule. This sparked distrust and hatred between the Arabs and Jews.

Today several million Palestinians live in Gaza and the West Bank, two areas seized by Israel in 1967. These areas are now ruled by the Palestinian Authority, though the Israeli government still controls life there. The tension between the two sides continues. Israel also faces the threat of war from Arabs in neighboring countries, such as Lebanon. The young people of Israel must continually deal with the stress of living in a country filled with conflict and surrounded by enemies.

When Israeli missiles destroyed a Palestinian school in Gaza in 2005, students attended class in a tent outside their former classroom.

Religious girls tend to dress conservatively, covering most of their bodies.

2 From High-Rises to Farms

IT IS DIFFICULT TO DESCRIBE THE DAILY LIVES OF ISRAEL'S TEENS, because their backgrounds have given them widely varied experiences. Jews from six continents have come to Israel since the country's founding. They reflect diverse cultures and hold various religious beliefs—or none at all. Added to the mix are the Israeli Arabs, descendants of the Arabs who lived in Israel before its founding. Although most Arabs are Muslim, some are Christian.

European immigrants who are not Jewish also live in Israel, mostly Eastern Europeans who came with Jewish spouses. In 2000, Russian non-Jews numbered more than 250,000. In addition, there are small minority groups with their own distinct cultures.

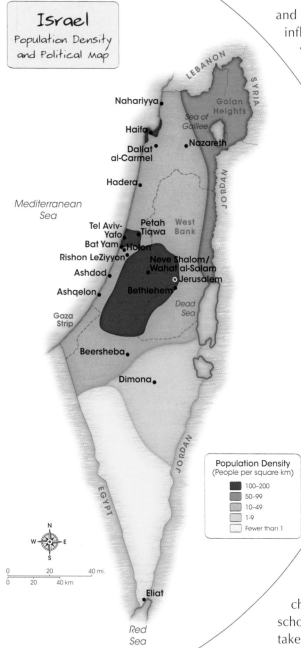

Israel
Population Density and Political Map

LEBANON

Nahariyya

Golan
Heights

Sea of
Galilee

Haifa

Daliat
al-Carmel

Nazareth

SYRIA

JORDAN

Hadera

Mediterranean
Sea

Tel Aviv-
Yafo

Petah
Tiqwa

West
Bank

Bat Yam

Holon

Rishon LeZiyyon

Ashdod

Neve Shalom/
Wahat al-Salam

Jerusalem

Ashqelon

Bethlehem

Dead
Sea

Gaza
Strip

Beersheba

Dimona

JORDAN

Population Density
(People per square km)

- 100–200
- 50–99
- 10–49
- 1–9
- Fewer than 1

EGYPT

N
W E
S

| 0 | 20 | 40 mi. |
| 0 | 20 | 40 km |

Eliat

Red
Sea

For teenagers, their family's ethnic and religious background not only influence what they do for fun and whom they spend their free time with; it can also shape their future path in schooling and the work force.

An Urban Lifestyle

Whatever their ethnic background or religion, most Israeli teens live in or near large, modern cities. More than 90 percent of the population is considered urban, and more than half the people live in just three cities— Tel Aviv, Jerusalem, and Haifa.

The largest urban area is Tel Aviv, a bustling center for business and the arts located on the Mediterranean Sea. Teens and their families might live in high-rise apartments in the heart of the city or single-family homes in the suburbs. Streets are crowded with cars, taxis, scooters, and bikes, and children can also take buses to go to school or visit friends. Some prefer to take a *monit-sherut,* a type of minibus.

The Azrieli Towers rise above much of Tel Aviv. Together they make up the largest commercial center in the Middle East.

monit-sherut

moh-NEET sheh-ROOT

These vehicles tend to be safer than large public buses, which are sometimes the target of terrorists. A train runs through the city and goes to nearby communities as well.

Jerusalem, the capital of Israel, has a history that dates back more than 3,000 years. The city has holy sites for three faiths: Judaism, Christianity, and Islam. The ultra-Orthodox community is especially large in Jerusalem, because

The Arabs of Israel

The founding of Israel in 1948 led to a war with its Arab neighbors. Over the next two years, between 600,000 and 750,000 Arabs living in Israel fled the country or were forced out by the Israeli military. About 150,000 remained behind. Today more than 1.5 million Arabs live in Israel. Some call themselves Palestinians, and feel connected to the Palestinians who live in the West Bank and Gaza. Others say they are Arab Israelis.

Just as Israeli Jews can be secular or religious, the Arabs split along religious lines. About 80 percent are Sunni Muslims. The Sunni are the largest Islamic group in the world. Like all Muslims, they follow the teachings of the Qur'an, the holy book of their faith, Islam. They believe the Qur'an was written by Muhammad, the founder of their faith. Muslims call God Allah and say he is the same God worshipped by Christians and Jews. But they believe that only people who live according to the Qur'an are the true followers of Allah.

A smaller number of Arabs in Israel, about 170,000, are Christian. Christianity gained followers in Palestine and other parts of the Middle East before the rise of Islam. The Israeli Christians are split into various faiths: Protestant, Roman Catholic, and Orthodox Catholic. Nazareth, the town where Jesus spent most of his life, is the largest Christian community in Israel.

Also among the Arabs of Israel are two smaller, distinct groups—the Bedouin and the Druze. The Bedouin are Muslims who trace their roots to nomads who roamed the desert of Israel for centuries, herding camels and sheep.

The Druze are the smallest group of Arabs in Israel. They are defined by their religion, which sprang from Islam. Its teachings, however, are kept from outsiders, and the Druze have strict rules for themselves. They can only marry each other. If a young Druze marries a Jew, Christian, or Arab, he or she is forced out of the community. The largest Druze town is Daliat al-Carmel, located in the Carmel Mountains not far from Haifa.

The Bedouin lifestyle is changing as aspects of modern life enter the culture.

Jerusalem's Old City is divided into four neighborhoods: the Armenian Quarter, Christian Quarter, Jewish Quarter, and Muslim Quarter.

families want to be close to the many yeshivot and the holiest places of their religion. The city is divided into the Old City and the New City. East Jerusalem, which was once part of the neighboring country of Jordan, is largely Arab, though more Jewish residents have settled there in recent years.

Daily life in the cities of Israel is similar to urban life around the world. Teens have typical chores, such as cleaning their rooms and doing the dishes. In some cases, parents give them allowances for doing the chores, but other parents give their kids money without expecting them to work for it.

In cities and towns, the lifestyle of teens varies, depending on their background. Many Ashkenazi teens benefit from the position of power their families have long held. The teens live in modern homes and enjoy easy access to computers, cell phones, and other advanced technology. The children of more successful Mizrahim also share these comforts.

Haredi girls do not let their religion's rules on dress keep them from enjoying time at the beach.

Religion is also a major factor in shaping how Israeli teens live. Haredi children, as well as adults, typically wear black clothing. Girls' bodies are covered almost entirely when they go out in public. Boys and men wear black hats and grow *peyot,* long curls of hair on each side of their heads. Despite their traditional dress, worn for centuries in their communities, haredi teens are not completely shut off from the modern world. They can listen to certain stations on the radio, and some are allowed to watch DVDs.

Like teens of other religions, young Druze sometimes feel limited by their faith's rules. Druze of all ages are not allowed to drink, smoke, or swear. Contact between unrelated men and women is limited. Yet the Druze are not cut off from modern things. The homes in the Druze community Daliat al-Carmel have satellite dishes on the roofs, and people freely use cell phones. Some Druze feel caught between the Arab and Jewish cultures around them, but they remain loyal to Israel. A young Druze named Amid

peyot
pe-YOHT

Zahar said, "Things are good for me here, very good for me ... I'm Israeli through and through."

For Muslims, prayer is an important part of daily life. Five times a day, Arab Israelis who practice Islam stop what they are doing so they can face Mecca, Islam's holiest city, and pray. Devout females, including young girls, cover their heads with a special scarf called a *hijab*. Muslims who are devoted to their faith have built schools to teach the Qur'an, Islam's holy text. The most extreme Muslims believe Israel does not have a right to exist. According to their understanding of the Qur'an and Arab

hijab
hih-JAHB

One way that the Druze reach out to others is through an international olive oil soap business that was started by a Druze grandmother in 1999.

The Smallest Minority

During the 19th century, a people called the Circassians were forced out of their homeland in the Caucasus Mountains in Russia. Many were Muslims, and they ended up in the military of the Ottoman Empire—an Islamic nation in what is now Turkey. During the 1870s, the Ottoman ruler sent some of the Circassians to Palestine, which was part of the empire at that time. Today about 3,000 of these non-Arab Muslims live in Israel, in two villages in the north.

Like the Druze, the Circassians serve in the Israeli Defense Forces. Their children attend their own schools, where they learn Hebrew and English, and speak their own language. Life in the two Circassian villages tends to be quiet. A visitor to one of these towns, Rihania, said teens "entertain themselves by driving around and around the narrow streets" on all-terrain vehicles. The Circassians, young and old, are proud that they have kept their culture alive in Israel.

history, all the land in Israel belongs to the Muslims. These extreme beliefs sometimes lead Muslim teens in Israel and the Palestinian-governed areas of the West Bank and Gaza to carry out acts of terrorism against Jewish Israelis. Teenagers as well as adults are killed in the terrorist attacks, which sometimes kill non-Jews as well.

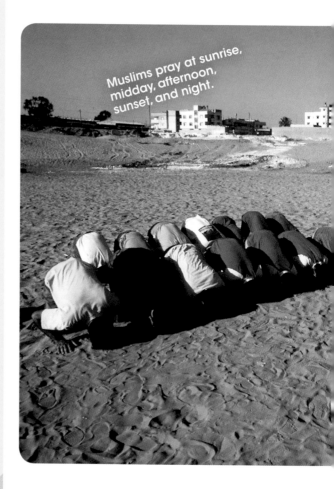

Muslims pray at sunrise, midday, afternoon, sunset, and night.

Life in the Country

The small rural population of Israel lives in villages scattered on the edges of the country. Few people live in the south, where the Negev Desert dominates the landscape. More than half of Israel's 140,000 Bedouin live in villages close to their traditional lands near the Negev. A few still live in tents, which were once a symbol of the Bedouin's tendency to move freely across the

Living Together

Arab Israelis can live wherever they want in Israel. Most, however, choose to live in strictly Arab communities, although some mostly Jewish cities have Arab neighborhoods. And in the city of Haifa, Jews, Muslims, and Christians live side by side. Yasser Mansour, an Arab Muslim doctor, chose to raise his family in Haifa because he said he saw it as an "island of sanity" in Israel. The various ethnic and religious groups have been able to live together peacefully. About 20 percent of the students at the university there are Muslims, more than at any other university in Israel. Haifa is also the home of the Baha'i headquarters. The Baha'i faith grew out of Islam but is now a separate religion, practiced mostly in India, Iran, and the United States.

Members of kibbutzim come together to celebrate harvest in September or October.

desert region. Small villages are also common in the north. Most residents of the villages are Arabs, and poverty tends to be high in the rural areas, because jobs are scarce.

In the Negev and other rural areas, Jewish Israelis have built special communities called *kibbutzim*. The first were founded before 1948, when Israel became a nation. In the past, families on a kibbutz, the name for one such community, worked and ate together and owned all property together. Children did not stay with their parents. Once they were 3 weeks old, they were placed in special "children's homes" and raised together, as if they were all part of the same family. Today the children's houses are gone, and parents raise their own children. But the kibbutzim still stress sharing and living together as much as possible.

Ongy Zisling was one of the first children to grow up with his parents at Kibbutz Ein Harod. A few years ago, the teenager told a U.S. journalist that "the kibbutz is a great place to grow up, a big family. No matter what happens, everybody is there for you." Today, however, a large number of children—about 70 percent at Ein Harod—leave the kibbutzim when they become adults.

kibbutzim
kee-buh-TSIM

A Day on the Kibbutz

The workers at a kibbutz—residents and volunteers—often spend many hours in the fields. Here is a typical schedule for one kibbutz:

5:15 A.M.	Wake up
5:30 A.M.	Leave for work site on farm
5:40 A.M.	Coffee or tea in the field
8:00 A.M.	Break for breakfast
8:50 A.M.	Back to work
12:00 P.M.	Lunch
12:30 P.M.	Back to work
2:00 P.M.	End of the work day; free time
6:00 P.M.	Dinner

Another group of rural Jewish residents in Israel are the settlers of the West Bank. This area between Israel and Jordan lies on the western bank of the Jordan River. After its 1967 war against Egypt, Syria, and Jordan, Israel took control of land that had been part of the biblical Israel—what Israelis call Eretz Israel. Ultra-Orthodox Jews led the push to settle in these lands, believing God had given them to the Jews. The settlers often took land that belonged to Palestinians, who wanted their own homeland in the region. In 2004, there were 187,000 Jewish settlers in the West Bank, which Israel's Orthodox citizens call by its biblical name, Judea and Samaria. Both religious and secular Jews have chosen to live there.

Some West Bank settlers live in fairly large towns in modern housing. Others live in trailer homes in villages with just a few dozen people. Money from the Israeli government helps pay for their housing and schools. Children in the region try to live normal lives, but the risk of violence is high. At times,

Homes in Jewish settlements in the West Bank are known for having red tile roofs.

Young Palestinians often become involved in clashes against Israeli military forces.

Food ... A Shared Part of Life

Despite the differences among the people of Israel, they share a love of native foods. Dates and olives are just two of the items that have been grown in Israel for thousands of years and are still enjoyed today. But the tables of Israel's dining rooms and restaurants are also filled with foods from around the world. The variety of foods reflects the immigrant background of the country's diverse population.

Some of the most common foods eaten in Israel are well known in other cultures, thanks to the growth of Middle Eastern restaurants. Hummus, a mixture of chickpeas and tahini—ground sesame seeds—is a favorite of Israeli Jews and Arabs alike. Falafels, deep-fried balls of chickpeas and spices, are another

Palestinians attack Jewish residents of the West Bank. Some ultra-Orthodox teens have also used violence to protest Israel's policy of closing some settlements in the West Bank. In 2006, a teenager named Avi described himself as a religious person and a good student. Yet he was willing to join other teens in throwing rocks and bottles at police sent to force Jewish residents from the settlements. "My parents are very scared of what I am doing," Avi said.

The situation in the West Bank, however, is not typical. Teens in a city such as Tel Aviv rarely see any signs of violence. Orr Redko, an 18-year-old Israeli American, said, "Los Angeles is far more dangerous than Israel." He does not feel threatened or fearful in his new home.

A vegetable market in Jerusalem's Old City sits under vaulted chambers that were built more than 1,000 years ago.

favorite and are sold on street corners across the country. A common Middle Eastern spice used in Israel is *za'atar*. This mixture of oregano, sumac, thyme, and sesame seeds is sometime sprinkled on flat pita bread. A Druze mother told cookbook author Joan Nathan that her family often gave za'atar to children in the morning, because "Za'atar opens up our minds and makes us more alert as students."

za'atar
ZAH-ah-TAHR

Breakfast in Israel is usually a simple meal such as eggs served with pita bread and milk. Israelis typically eat a fancier breakfast on their Sabbath day. The morning meal on the holy day is

Vegetable-filled salads are offered in a typical breakfast buffet.

more likely to include pastries, while Arabs enjoy a type of pancake called a *kataif*, which can be stuffed with nuts or cream. When entertaining, Israelis like to offer their guests large breakfast buffets that feature cheeses, salads, and breads.

Lunch, served around noon, is often the biggest meal of the day, and some teens go home to eat it with their families. Many of these meals start with an assortment of dips, spreads, and salads, eaten with pita bread. This course is called the *mezze*, and

kataif
kah-TAYF

mezze
MEH-zeh

Religion & Food

kashrut
kahsh-ROOT

As with so many parts of life in Israel, religion affects food. According to the Torah, God said the Jews could not eat certain animals, including pigs, rabbits, and shellfish. They also could not eat the blood of any animal they killed. These and other food laws are called *kashrut*. In English, following these laws is called keeping kosher. Animals must be killed and drained of their blood in a certain way, and meat and dairy products cannot be eaten together, or even touch the same plates. Muslims follow similar rules about not eating pork or blood. Not all Israelis keep kosher, and restaurants can serve non-kosher foods. Israeli teens have their choice of sharing a snack or meal with friends at either a kosher or non-kosher McDonald's. The kosher ones do not serve milk shakes (because they serve hamburgers) and are closed on the Sabbath and religious holidays.

Kosher McDonald's are clearly labeled in English and Hebrew.

it features foods eaten throughout the Middle East, such as hummus, eggplant dishes, and a salad called tabbouleh. For their main meal, Israelis enjoy beef, lamb, poultry, or fish, along with breads, salads, and vegetables. Dinner tends to be a lighter meal, featuring eggs, dairy products, and salads.

Israel does not have a national dish or style of cooking. Its cooks' ethnic backgrounds influence what is served. Dishes that settlers brought from Europe include potato latkes, a kind of pancake, and *gefilte*—a dish made from chopped fish.

A popular dessert is figs served in syrup.

Mizrahim from Morocco make a stew called *tagine*, usually served with the grain couscous. Italian Jews are known for dishes that feature fish cooked with spices or sauces, and Russian Jews enjoy borscht—a beet soup—and smoked fish.

Israelis of all backgrounds enjoy desserts. A common Middle Eastern

gefilte
geh-FEEL-teh

tagine
tah-JEEN

dessert is *baklawa*, made from pastry dough, nuts, and sugar. A similar dessert, called *kinaffeh*, is stuffed with cheese and nuts. European-based desserts include pastries and cakes made with apples, which are grown in the orchards of northern Israel. Israel's families enjoy the wide variety of foods their country produces.

baklawa
bah-klah-WAH

kinaffeh
kih-NAH-feh

Many of the sauces served in the mezze course are spicy.

The average family size is two or three children.

3 Family Roles & Friendships

AS PART OF THEIR SCHOOLING, most Jewish Israeli students explore their families' history, including how and why they came to Israel. For some Ashkenazi, the project teaches them about the Holocaust, the German Nazis' attempt during World War II to kill all the Jews of Europe. Many Jews who survived the Holocaust helped build the modern nation of Israel.

Mizrahi children come from families that once lived in Arab countries of the Middle East and North Africa. These students learn about the mass emigration of 870,000 Arab Jews during and after various wars Israel fought with Arab neighbors.

The family-history projects help students learn about the Jewish people's difficult past. During that history, families have played an important part in keeping Jewish traditions alive. At times, the Jews could not worship in public, so private services were held in homes. Strong family ties helped the Jews practice their faith and survive the prejudice they often faced from non-Jews.

The Jewish People

Mizrahi children from Yemen

Their shared religion and history of facing prejudice helps unite Jews, yet differences in backgrounds exist. Here's a look at some of the various groups of Jewish people in Israel.

Ashkenazim

Ashkenazim are Jews who lived in Europe before coming to Israel. Several major waves of Ashkenazim have come to Israel, starting with the first Zionists more than 120 years ago. But the largest resettlement of European Jews happened right after the founding of modern Israel, when several hundred thousand arrived from 1948 to 1951. Secular Ashkenazim created modern Israel and still dominate major businesses and politics. The Ashkenazim also include religious Jews, from haredim to Reformed, the least restrictive branch of Judaism.

Mizrahim

The Jews who came to Israel from Islamic countries are called Mizrahim. Some had settled in Israel when the land was still called Palestine, and hundreds of thousands of Mizrahim came in the years after Israel's founding. To some Ashkenazim, the Mizahim sometimes seemed more Arab than Jewish—they spoke Arabic, ate Arab foods, and tended to have darker skin. The Mizrahim were also more religious than the secular founders of Israel. Their traditional religious beliefs seemed to threaten the modern democratic state that the Ashkenazim hoped to build. Those fears led to prejudice against the Mizrahim, who faced decades of living in crowded neighborhoods and taking low-paying jobs. By the 1960s, however, the Mizrahim made up 60 percent of Israel's population and were firmly part of the country's native Jewish population.

Sephardim

Starting more than 1,000 years ago, Jews settled in large numbers in the areas that are now Spain and Portugal. These Jews came to be called Sephardim, from the Hebrew word S'farad—"Spain." Beginning in the 1490s, many of the Sephardim scattered across Europe as Spain's Roman Catholic rulers clamped down on the open practice of Judaism. Some Sephardim also went to the Middle East and Asia. Today the Sephardim are distinct from the Ashkenazim, who do not have roots in Spain. They are also distinct from most Mizharim, even though the two groups often lived near each other in North Africa and the Middle East. The Mizrahim and Sephardim traditionally spoke different languages and used different prayers.

Russian Immigrants

A large wave of European immigrants came to Israel during the 1990s, when the Soviet Union broke apart. (The Soviet Union included Russia and other now-independent nations in Eastern Europe and Central Asia.) The Russian immigrants now make up 15 percent of Israel's population, and they are still struggling to adjust to life in their new land. Most do not speak Hebrew, though their children are learning it. Parents who received good educations in the former Soviet Union often have trouble finding jobs to match their skills. Experts, however, think the sheer number of Russian Jews in Israel will give them greater political power in the years to come. They are mostly secular and so might curb some of the power of the religious Jews in Israel.

The Ethiopian Jews

Distinct from the Mizrahim of North Africa are the Jews of Ethiopia. For almost 2,000 years, the Jews of Ethiopia, an East African nation, were largely cut off from other Jews and the outside world. These Jews faced difficult living conditions in their homeland. In 1984 the Israeli government began to fly thousands of them out of Ethiopia and into Israel. Today about 80,000 of these so-called "lost" Jews live in Israel. Most arrived speaking only Amharic, the language of Jews in Ethiopia, and were largely unschooled rural farmers. They had trouble finding jobs and adjusting to urban life. Today about 6 percent of Ethiopian teens drop out of high school—higher than the national average. And Ethiopian teens are twice as likely as other Israeli youth to get into legal trouble. But the Ethiopian community is slowly adapting to life in Israel.

A young Russian immigrant arrives at an Israeli airport.

Families, Marriage, & Divorce

Family ties remain important in Israel, and Jewish Israelis are likely to place their family above their work or other interests. The non-Jews of Israel also tend to have strong family ties, though family life for Arab Israelis has changed over time. Before 1948, an Arab household often included a husband and wife, their young children, and adult sons and their families. Today only about one in 10 Arab Israeli households includes more than one family. More common is the nuclear family of a husband, wife, and young children.

Arab families once had many children, but now more parents are choosing to have smaller families. With fewer children, one mother explained, "I can give each of them more education and a good life." The haredim of Israel usually have more children than do secular Jewish families; Orthodox Jews believe God welcomes large families.

Under Israeli law, a marriage between two Jews must be performed by an Orthodox rabbi, a Jewish spiritual

Jewish families commonly enjoy dinner together on Friday evening, which marks the start of their Sabbath.

The average haredi family has seven or eight children.

Becoming an Israeli Citizen

In 1950, Israel's lawmakers passed a law regarding who could become a citizen. The Law of Return said any Jew living anywhere in the world could come to Israel and receive citizenship. Later the law was changed to say people who converted to Judaism could also come to Israel and become citizens. Non-Jewish spouses of Jews can also receive citizenship.

The law declared that Israel was a home to all Jewish people throughout the world. It welcomed all Jews to return to the ancient homeland.

leader. A rabbi also has to give his permission for a couple to divorce, and the husband must sign a document called a *get*. If he refuses to sign the get, a wife cannot get a divorce. Orthodox religious law, which applies to all Israelis, says that a Jewish person cannot marry a non-Jew. A child of a mixed marriage—one Jew and one non-Jew—may or may not be considered Jewish. According to Jewish law, children must have Jewish mothers to be considered Jewish. Religious law also governs the marriages of Muslims and Christians.

get
geht

41

The Bedouin Family

In the Bedouin family, the focus has traditionally been on the son. Until the 1960s, girls rarely went to school beyond fifth grade. They were expected to stay home and help their mothers. This attitude is changing, however, as the Bedouin adopt a more urban lifestyle.

At one time, the number of Bedouin who could read was just 5 percent of the population. Today more than 75 percent can read, and most who can't are over the age of 55.

Parents & Children

As with so many parts of life, family relations, and sometimes even friendships, are influenced by religious and ethnic backgrounds. Secular Israeli parents tend to give their children a significant amount of freedom. Teens in Tel Aviv might be allowed out on their own until well after midnight—unless they have school the next day. Micaela Terk, 14, said, "I tell my mom where I'm going … and where I'm staying. She trusts me to take care of myself, and I do." In general, Israeli parents encourage their teens to be independent.

For haredi teens, life is not as free.

It is not common to see secular and religious teens interacting in public.

Common Names in Israel

HEBREW	
Boys	**Girls**
Ari	Dana
David	Meirav
Gil	Noa
Moshe	Shira
Yossi	Tal

ARABIC	
Boys	**Girls**
Ali	Alina
Fareed	Fatima
Ismael	Salwa
Khaled	Yasmin
Muhammad	Zaara

According to their religious beliefs, boys and girls must be separated in public places. Haredi teens don't date, and marriages are usually arranged by their parents, who use professionals to find spouses. Their families' religious beliefs also influence what they will do with their lives. Haredi parents expect their daughters to marry young and begin having large families, while the boys are expected to study the Torah—and perhaps do little else—for their whole lives.

Ultra-Orthodox children are often kept separate from secular kids. A haredi teenager told a reporter, "My father wants me to have friends who believe like us."

Yet Amira Feldman, a secular teen, said a religious boy was one of her best friends. She said, "His parents . . . were a little taken aback that his best friend was a secular girl, but when they got to know me, they got used to the idea, and now they have no problem with it."

Haredi teens have some contact with secular Jews at weddings and other social events. Some young haredim are tempted by the secular lifestyle of movies and dating and popular music. A few decide to leave their families and seek help from secular Jews in adopting more modern ways. On the

Though some family members leave the Orthodox lifestyle, they may keep close ties with their family.

other hand, some secular Jews find the Orthodox life appealing. They welcome the order and discipline it demands, so they leave their families to pursue the religious life. Haredim also have close relations with their neighbors, and families help each other whenever they can. This friendliness is also appealing to some secular Jews.

Contact between young Arab and Jewish Israelis is also limited. If they attend the same schools, they are not likely to hang out with each other after class. Dating between the two groups is also rare.

Mizrahi writer Loolwa Khazzoom described her experiences as a college student dating a Bedouin Arab. She welcomed the similarities between her culture and her boyfriend's. They enjoyed similar foods, and both cultures warmly welcomed guests into their homes. But a Jewish friend warned Khazzoom that her Arab boyfriend would slit her throat. Because of the hatred between many Arabs and Jews, it's not usually easy for teens from the two groups to interact.

The distinct religious and ethnic divisions within Israel make it hard for teens of different groups to get to know each other. Military service brings people of different backgrounds together—so does attending a college or university. But in some ways, as the Israeli government describes it, the country remains a mosaic. This kind of artwork is made from many tiny colored tiles that are placed near each other to create an image. Each religious or ethnic group in Israel is a separate tile. But taken together, they create the state of Israel.

Bringing Teens Together

One group working to build friendships between young Israeli Jews and Arabs is Peace Child Israel. Founded in 1988, Peace Child uses arts, especially theater, to bring Jews and Arabs together. The teens write songs and plays in both Hebrew and Arabic, and some have been invited to Europe and North America to perform their work. Omaima Khalifa, an Arab who was part of Peace Child in 2002, told a Jerusalem newspaper, "The most important lesson I learned from Peace Child Israel is that change is always possible"

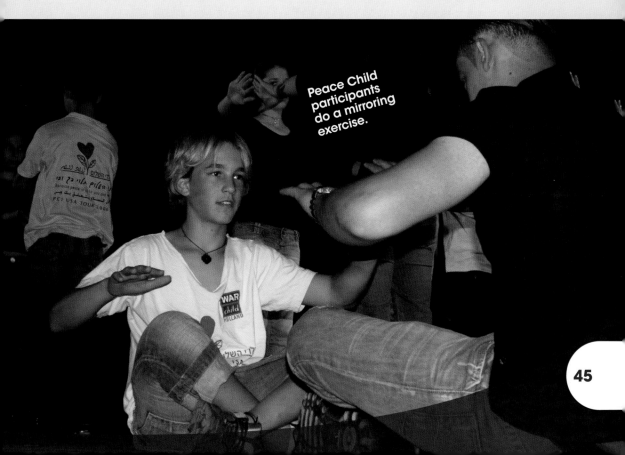

Peace Child participants do a mirroring exercise.

Dressing in costume for Purim draws connections to themes of mistaken identity in the story of Queen Esther, the holiday's honoree.

4 Honoring God & Country

THE JEWISH HOLIDAY OF PURIM CALLS FOR MERRIMENT, AND ISRAELIS CELEBRATE IN STYLE. Booths line the street, selling food to eat and offering games to play. Adults and children wear masks and costumes, and everywhere people are laughing. Falling in February or March, Purim honors the heroics of Esther, a Jewish queen who saved her people from massacre in Persia more than 2,500 years ago.

Purim is one of many Jewish holidays celebrated in Israel, but none is as light-hearted as this one. Many of the holidays mark solemn occasions in Jewish history, or ask Jews to examine their lives and their relationships with God. Still, Israelis celebrate joyously at other events, such as weddings and bar mitzvahs. The country's Muslims and Christians also have their own religious holidays and personal celebrations.

The Jewish Calendar

Israeli students learn how to use at least two calendars. The official calendar is the Jewish calendar, which is based on the movement of the moon around Earth. Students also learn the Gregorian calendar—the one used in Europe and the United States—and its dates appear on some documents. For example, on its Web site, the Israeli newspaper *Haaretz* uses both calendar systems to post the date. The Gregorian calendar is solar—based on the movement of Earth around the sun. In moon-based, or lunar, calendars there are 12.4 months for every 12 months on a solar calendar. This difference leads to the appearance of a "leap month" in some years in Israel. It also explains why most Jewish holidays do not fall on a set date on the Gregorian calendar. Although Nissan is considered the first month of the calendar, the year changes during Tishri at Rosh Hashana. Arabs also use their own calendar, which is also based on the cycles of the moon.

Name of Jewish month	Order in calendar	Number of days	Place on Gregorian calendar
Nissan	1	30	March-April
Iyar	2	29	April-May
Sivan	3	30	May-June
Tammuz	4	29	June-July
Av	5	30	July-August
Elul	6	29	August-September
Tishri	7	30	September-October
Cheshvan	8	29 or 30	October-November
Kislev	9	29 or 30	November-December
Tevet	10	29	December-January
Shevat	11	30	January-February
Adar I (leap years only)	12	30	February-March
Adar (called Adar II in leap years)	12 (13 in leap years)	29	February-March

Major Jewish & Secular Holidays

Rosh Hashana (New Year's)	September-October
Yom Kippur	September-October
Sukkot	September-October
Simhat Torah	October
Hanukkah	December
Purim	February-March
Passover	March-April
Holocaust Remembrance Day	March-April
Fallen Soldiers Remembrance Day	April-May
Independence Day	April-May
Shavuot	May-June

Days for Religion & History

In keeping with the Jewish calendar, the new year in Israel is celebrated in September or October. Rosh Hashana, as the holiday is called, is a religious observance that asks Jews to look forward to the year to come and think of ways they can improve their lives. After attending synagogue, religious Israelis go home for lavish meals with their families.

Most families have a tradition of serving various kinds of fruits and vegetables at the Rosh Hashana meal. Apple is dipped in honey, with the sweetness offering hope for a good new year. Round carrot slices are said to look like gold coins, a sign of future wealth. The tough-skinned pomegranates are said to have 613 seeds—the same number of good deeds the Torah says a Jew should perform during the year. In general, the Rosh Hashana foods are seen as symbols of hope for the new year.

Eight days after Rosh Hashanah is the most serious day of the year for religious Jews in Israel and around the

On Rosh Hashana, the shofar, a trumpet made from a ram's horn, is blown as part of religious observances.

49

world. On Yom Kippur, or the Day of Atonement, Jews fast and attend religious services the whole day. They ask God to forgive their sins from the past year. Even some secular Jews take part in this important day, which gives people time to reflect on how they live. For Yom Kippur, everything shuts down for 25 hours: radio and TV stations go off the air, roads are closed, and movie theaters and restaurants close their doors.

The major holiday season continues five days later with Sukkot, or the Feast of Tabernacles. Sukkot marks the Jews' exodus, or departure, from Egypt after having been held there as slaves 3,300 years ago. The festival also celebrates the harvest. In the period between Yom Kippur and Sukkot, Israeli families and businesses set up outdoor tents called tabernacles, similar to the ones the Jews lived in after leaving Egypt. Some modern Israelis live in their tents until Sukkot.

The major spring holiday in Israel is Passover. It marks the time in Egypt when God is thought to have spared the children of Jewish families, while killing the first-born children of the Egyptians. Passover, which lasts a week, also requires Jews to remember the suffering they endured in Egypt. As

During Sukkot, several rituals are carried out in the tents, including the beating of willow branches while reciting prayers.

HONORING GOD & COUNTRY

Orthodox Jews have a separate set of dishes, pots, and utensils that are purified and used just for Passover.

with Yom Kippur, many secular Jews take part in Passover activities.

The highlight of Passover is the Seder, a special meal featuring foods that the Israelites, the people of the ancient kingdom of Israel, are said to have eaten after leaving Egypt. A typical Seder includes all the members of the family and sometimes friends. Matzoh, a flat bread, is served because the Israelites did not have time to let their bread rise. Parsley is dipped in salt water. The parsley reflects the simple origins of the Jewish people, while the salt water stands for the tears they cried during their years of suffering. Children play a special role during the Seder, because they are chosen to ask four questions that explain why the Seder is so important to the Jews.

Children are the main focus of a lesser Jewish holiday, Hanukkah, or the Festival of Lights. This day remembers the heroics of the Maccabees, Jewish leaders who inspired the Jews of Palestine to revolt against their Greek rulers. Hanukkah lasts for eight days, and on each night, from one to eight candles are lit. Parents use Hanukkah as a time to give their kids gifts, and children play games with a dreidel, a special spinning toy. In Israel, schools close for Hanukkah, but businesses stay open.

In the spring, two secular holidays are honored: Independence Day and Fallen Soldiers Remembrance Day. Independence Day marks the founding of the modern state of Israel. A public ceremony includes the lighting of 12 torches, one for each of the original 12 tribes of Israel. Later towns and cities across the country light fireworks and hold public celebrations with music. The day before, Fallen Soldiers Remembrance Day, is a more somber occasion. Israelis use this holiday to remember the citizens who died fighting to create Israel and those who have died defending it since 1948.

Ask the Children

The questions and answers Jewish children recite during the Seder are called the Nah Mishtanah — "Why is [this night] different?" They are sung in Hebrew. The question is repeated three times, and the answers are given in this order:

On all other nights, we eat leavened products and matzoh, and on this night only matzoh.
On all other nights, we eat all vegetables, and on this night only bitter herbs.
On all other nights, we don't dip our food even once, and on this night we dip twice.
On all other nights, we eat sitting or reclining, and on this night we only recline.

Independence Day celebrations include parades with dancers and other performers.

Another holiday, Holocaust Remembrance Day, honors the Jews who died during World War II. For two minutes, a siren sounds and all Jewish Israelis across the country stop whatever they are doing. As 16-year-old Michael Kozakov put it, the day "unites the secular and religious people into one."

Islamic & Christian Holidays

In Israel, stores and streets are not closed on Islamic and Christian holidays, as they are

The 12 Tribes

Jacob was the grandson of Abraham, the founder of Judaisim. Jacob had 12 sons. Each was given his own territory in ancient Israel, and each was the founder of a tribe. The 12 sons after whom the tribes are named are:

Reuben
Levi
Zebulun
Dan
Asher
Joseph
Simeon
Judah
Issachar
Gad
Naphtali
Benjamin

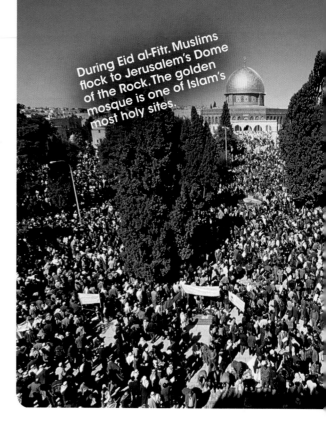
During Eid al-Fitr, Muslims flock to Jerusalem's Dome of the Rock. The golden mosque is one of Islam's most holy sites.

on the important secular and Jewish holidays. But the holidays are important to the people who celebrate them.

The most important Islamic holiday is Ramadan. During this monthlong celebration, Israeli Muslims fast while the sun is up, then eat their only meal at night. Ramadan starts in November and ends with a three-day feast called Eid al-Fitr. For this celebration, children eat sweets that their mothers baked and receive gifts from friends and family, such as coins. Like the Jews, the Muslims also have their own calendar and a separate New Year's celebration. Called Al-Hejira, the Islamic New Year marks Islam's founder Muhammad's trip in 622 to Medina, in what is now Saudi Arabia. There he set up the first Islamic government. The Islamic New Year's Day falls in either March or April.

For Christians, the main religious holidays are Christmas and Easter. For Protestants and Roman Catholics, the birth of Jesus Christ is celebrated at Christmas on December 25. Members of Orthodox churches celebrate the birth of Jesus Christ in January, both in Israel and around the world.

Since Israel is a Jewish nation, Christmas is not an official holiday, and stores and businesses stay open.

Easter is the Christian holiday that marks the rising of Christ after his death. On Good Friday, the day Jesus was killed, modern Christians fill

Religion in Israel

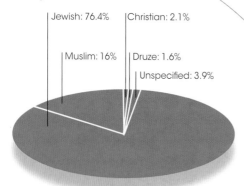

Jewish: 76.4% Christian: 2.1%

Muslim: 16% Druze: 1.6%

Unspecified: 3.9%

Source: United States Central Intelligence Agency.
The World Factbook—Israel.

the streets of Jerusalem, following the route Jesus walked on his last day. Israeli Christians and tourists also visit the towns of Bethlehem, where Jesus was born, and Nazareth, where he spent most of his life.

Private Celebrations

Jews have a special ceremony for young people to mark their passing into adulthood. The event, called a bar mitzvah (bat mitzvah for girls), happens when a boy turns 13 or a girl turns 12. The young adults read passages from the Torah. After the ceremony, the children, their relatives, and their guests have a huge feast, and the child having the bar

or bat mitzvah receives gifts. While the ceremony is usually in a synagogue, some Israelis hold their children's bar or bat mitzvah outdoors or at sacred sites.

Secular Jews in Israel—especially Russian immigrants—do not always follow the tradition of having a bar or bat mitzvah. But one type of private ceremony calls for a feast whether the people involved are religious or secular, Arab or Christian or Jewish. Weddings in Israel, as in most countries, are times of great celebration.

All Jews must be married by an Orthodox rabbi if they want to be married in Israel. Otherwise, they must leave the country and have a civil marriage.

One sacred site where bar and bat mitzvahs are held is Jerusalem's Western Wall, the only remains of Judaism's Second Temple.

55

In some Jewish weddings, the bride, along with her parents, lead a procession of musicians and guests to the ceremony.

About 30 percent of all couples marry outside the country, then usually return to Israel for a celebration. In a traditional Orthodox Jewish wedding, the bride and groom stand under a *huppa*, a piece of cloth attached to four poles. When the rabbi ends the ceremony, the groom smashes a glass, and the guests cry *"Mazel tov"*—"Good luck." Then the party begins with food and dancing. For haredim, the ceremony is slightly different. The bride wears a veil over her face, and she and her husband-to-be never touch. After the wedding, men and women dance and eat separately.

For Israel's Muslims, a traditional

huppa
hu-PAH

Mazel tov
ma-ZAHL tov

a *kitab*. (Jews sign a similar contract, called a *ketuba*.) With the legal part over, the new couple and their families begin a series of dinner feasts that can last for days. For religious Muslims, no alcohol is served, and the men and women celebrate separately.

kitab
kih-TAHB

ketuba
keh-tu-BAH

Marrying More than Once

When the Bible was written, Jewish men in ancient Palestine sometimes had two or more wives, a practice called polygamy. A few years after Israel was founded, it outlawed polygamy for Jews. The practice of polygamy among Jewish Israelis had ended centuries before, for the most part, but some immigrants from the countries of Iran and Yemen still had two wives. Polygamy is permitted by Islamic law, and today some Muslim men still marry more than one woman, though the government only considers one of the wives to be a legal partner.

wedding often starts with what seems like a parade. Guests sing and beat drums and tambourines, while the bride and the rest of the wedding party arrive in rows of cars. An Islamic marriage does not require the bride to be present. Her father, or another male, conducts a ceremony with the groom and other men, followed by the signing of a contract called

57

Following high school, the majority of Israeli teens serve in the Israeli Defense Forces, the country's military.

5 From Farms to Factories

TEENS IN ISRAEL CAN LOOK FORWARD TO WORKING IN ANY ONE OF A NUMBER OF INTERESTING AND CHALLENGING INDUSTRIES. From technology-based jobs, such as software development, to service positions, such as banking or retail sales, Israel is home to a wide variety of work.

Some young Israelis get an introduction to the working world while still in high school. The service industry, which employs 75 percent of Israelis, provides teens with part-time positions at stores, cafes, or restaurants. Legally teens can work at age 15, though they can work at family businesses before then.

A Glittering Industry

Cutting and polishing diamonds is an old craft. For centuries, Jews living in Antwerp, Belgium, were some of the best diamond cutters in the world. The trade and, eventually, businesses have been passed down through family generations. Now the diamond industry is a key part of the Israeli economy. But even with diamonds, high-tech methods play a part. Lasers and computers have made it easier to cut diamonds more precisely than in the past. Israel has the world's largest polished diamond industry, selling more than U.S.$6 billion worth of stones each year.

Israel is the world leader in the exporting of cut and polished diamonds.

OVADIA DIAM
Manufacturer of Triangles, Heart
New Diamond Tower, Suite 974, 3A Jabot
Tel: 972-3-5752388, 6130580, Fax: 972-

After completing high school, some teens will delay their entry into full-time work and begin college. Students who pass their bagrut exams can go to one of the country's eight universities or study abroad. Smaller colleges are spread out across Israel, and several focus on one area of study, such as engineering, technology, or the arts. Israel also has separate colleges to train teachers.

Military Service

For most young Israelis, however, college is not the first stop after high school. At 18, all Jewish, Druze, and Circassian men begin a mandatory three-year term in the Israeli Defense Forces (IDF). Women, too, serve at least 21 months. Arabs, whether Christian or Muslim, can volunteer for military service.

Young Israelis see military service as a way to help their country. Their service also has practical benefits. At 16, Ben Argeband saw his future military duty as "a learning experience, and a place where, I'm sure, I will meet my greatest and closest friends for life."

Military service, however, has obvious dangers. The threat of war is real, and terrorist attacks are a part of life. Young Israeli soldiers barely out of high school face harsh realities. Liron Heffetz was just 19 when he was on duty driving a tank through the Gaza Strip, home to many Palestinians. His orders were to drive through a local farmer's field where terrorists might hide.

Women on the Battlefield

Israeli women—unlike those in most other countries—can join combat units, putting them directly into the action on the battlefield. One unit of Israeli ground soldiers, for example, is 80 percent female. Women who want to be officers must complete a difficult 17-week training session. The cadets practice shooting, fight hand-to-hand, and learn how to take apart and put back together their Uzi machine guns—while blindfolded. About a dozen women have also completed the Israeli Air Force's course for jet pilots, with three of them trained to fly combat missions. In 2006, the Israeli Defense Force said it would increase the number of combat jobs available to women.

Young volunteers often help with community projects, including social events for young children.

Heffetz did not like the idea of destroying the farmer's only source of money. But, he later said, "I decided that Israeli lives are worth more than a field." Other young soldiers must bury their friends who die from terrorist attacks, then quickly return to their duty. When the soldiers' military service is over, the challenges of finding a job or going to college seem small compared with what they have seen and done while defending their nation.

Giving to Others

The Israeli government allows young people to put off their military service for one year to do volunteer work. Each year a few thousand graduating high school seniors do so, often living together in communities called communes. Some work in poor villages, helping the children with schoolwork or organizing social activities. Tomer Reingwertz was 18 when he entered his volunteer service working with children.

He said, "I believe that the connection with the youth is important, that there is a way to change the world."

Some Israeli youth volunteer to work overseas. In 2006, Benyamin Zinshtein traveled to the United States to live with an American Jewish family. His goal was to create an understanding between Jews in Israel and the United States. During his time in Connecticut, Benyamin taught Hebrew to children. He said his time as a volunteer made him "more independent" and better able to "think for myself."

Although teens like Tomer and Benyamin will go on to serve in the IDF, some Israelis are allowed to do volunteer work instead of serving in the military. Since 1971, religious girls have been able to join National Service, Israel's national volunteer program. Ultra-Orthodox leaders didn't want religious girls to serve with men in the military, so National Service was a compromise that lets them still do something useful for their country. Some National Service programs have been created for other Israeli teens who don't enter the military for medical or moral reasons.

In 2005, about 300 Israeli teens decided to take a drastic step to protest military service. They wrote government officials and said they would not join the IDF because they opposed Israel's policies toward the Palestinians in Gaza and the West Bank. The teens became known as "refuseniks." When they are called to serve, the teens explain why they are conscientious objectors—people morally opposed to war and killing. Eyal Brami was one refusenik who went to jail for his beliefs. In 2005 he wrote, "I cannot take part in [Israeli] military activities, due to the criminal, immoral and blind behavior of the Israeli Defense Force." After 78 days in a military prison, he was released.

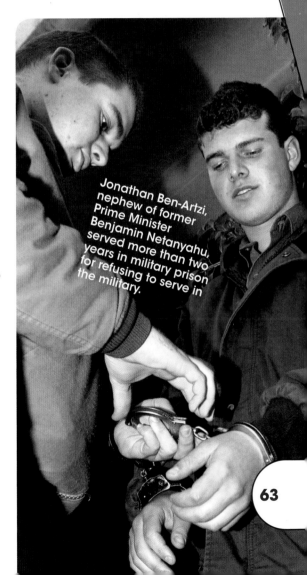

Jonathan Ben-Artzi, nephew of former Prime Minister Benjamin Netanyahu, served more than two years in military prison for refusing to serve in the military.

Refuseniks and conscientious objectors, however, are a small part of the Israeli teenage population. The majority of Israeli teens see military service as an important duty—as well as a way to gain skills and make connections that help them later in life.

Israel's Technology Industry

Among the skills teens acquire during military service are those needed for technology-based jobs. For example, Gil Shwed, the founder of an international security software development company named Check Point,

Robot-Building Champs

For some Israelis, an interest in high technology starts in high school. For several years, some high schools have sent teams to the United States to compete in the annual Fire Fighting Home Robot Contest at Trinity College in Hartford, Connecticut. The robots have to detect and put out a lit candle after traveling through an arena made to look like the inside of a building. The skills learned for the contest come in handy for students who want to pursue careers in science and technology.

The military uses robotic equipment to handle suspicious items that may be bombs.

learned his software skills in the Israeli Defense Forces. After serving in the military, he didn't go to college. Instead, he went right into the software business. Other technology business executives learned their skills in the Mossad, the Israeli spy agency.

Technology & Teens

Israeli teens enjoy the modern benefits of technology as well. In their schools and in their homes, Israeli students are connected to the world. On their cell phones, Israelis are some of the world's biggest talkers, using on average of more than 300 minutes every month. Israeli teens use the Internet to do research, play games, and stay in touch with friends. According to a 2005 Israeli government survey, almost 90 percent of Israel's middle- and high-school-age boys surfed the Net every week, for almost six hours a week. Girls logged on at a slightly lower percentage—79 percent— and spent about three hours per week online. Arab students are less likely to get online than Jewish Israelis, perhaps a reflection of the economic differences between the two groups.

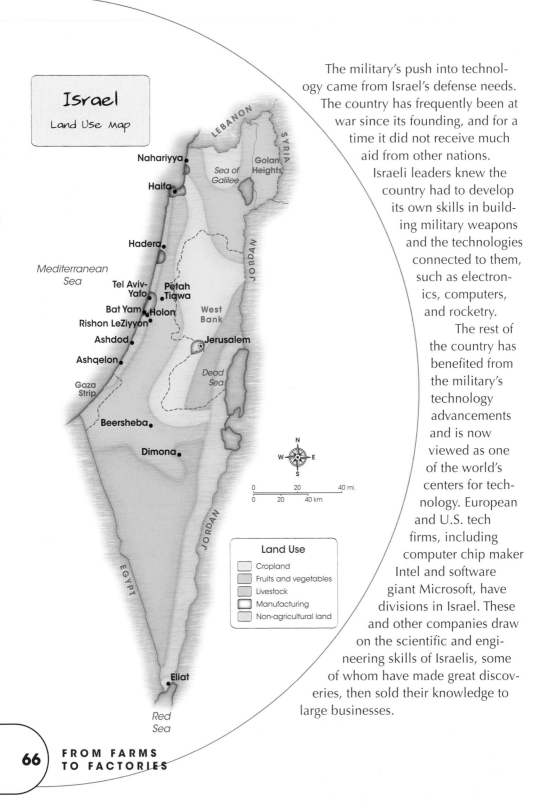

Israel
Land Use Map

LEBANON

Nahariyya

SYRIA

Golan Heights

Sea of Galilee

Haifa

Hadera

Mediterranean Sea

JORDAN

Tel Aviv-Yafo

Petah Tiqwa

Bat Yam

Holon

West Bank

Rishon LeZiyyon

Ashdod

Jerusalem

Ashqelon

Dead Sea

Gaza Strip

Beersheba

Dimona

N
W E
S

0   20   40 mi.
0   20   40 km

JORDAN

EGYPT

Land Use
- Cropland
- Fruits and vegetables
- Livestock
- Manufacturing
- Non-agricultural land

Eliat

Red Sea

The military's push into technology came from Israel's defense needs. The country has frequently been at war since its founding, and for a time it did not receive much aid from other nations.

Israeli leaders knew the country had to develop its own skills in building military weapons and the technologies connected to them, such as electronics, computers, and rocketry.

The rest of the country has benefited from the military's technology advancements and is now viewed as one of the world's centers for technology. European and U.S. tech firms, including computer chip maker Intel and software giant Microsoft, have divisions in Israel. These and other companies draw on the scientific and engineering skills of Israelis, some of whom have made great discoveries, then sold their knowledge to large businesses.

FROM FARMS TO FACTORIES

Technology reaches a wide range of Israeli industries, including agriculture. The push to improve farming methods began long before anyone knew the term "high tech." Starting in the late 19th century, Ashkenazi settlers began irrigating Israel's desert regions to grow crops. Those efforts increased as more kibbutzim appeared.

Israeli farmers used the irrigation and greenhouses to grow vegetables such as tomatoes and peppers, and fruit such as oranges, kiwis, and melons. One farm technology perfected in Israel was the drip method of irrigation. Small amounts of water are dripped directly into a plant's root system.

Today science plays a greater role on the farm, as scientists use their knowledge of genetics to produce plants able to grow with less water or requiring less pesticides to fight off bugs. In chicken coops, home computers are used to monitor and ensure

Similar to a kibbutz, a *moshav* is a cooperative farm where individual families retain ownership of their homes and farmland.

Division of Labor

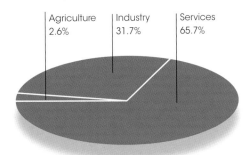

| Agriculture 2.6% | Industry 31.7% | Services 65.7% |

Source: United States Central Intelligence Agency. *The World Factbook—Israel.*

conditions are favorable for egg production. Israel's hens lay more eggs than chickens anywhere else in the world.

Farming, however, is not a realistic career choice for many Israeli teens. The growth of cities means less land is available to farm. Just 2 percent of Israeli workers are in agriculture. Even on the kibbutzim, most of the money made comes from non-farming sources, such as tourism and related services.

At its founding, Israel had almost no natural resources that could be sold to other countries. Farming provided one main export—flowers. Now, thanks to high tech, the Dead Sea contributes to Israel's exports. This sea got its name because its high levels of salt and other minerals make it impossible for plants and sea creatures to live in its waters. But those minerals are now important products for the Israeli economy.

During the 1980s and 1990s, scientists perfected new methods for removing some of the minerals from the water. One of the most important is the metal magnesium, which is used to make airplanes and engine parts. Another mineral produced in Israel is phosphate, which is found in the Negev Desert. It is used in certain kinds of soap. New methods for taking the mineral from the sandy desert helped spur Israel's phosphate industry.

The skilled work of scientists has also shaped Israel's medical industry. The country's largest company is Teva Pharmaceutical. Its main business is making generic drugs—medicines that are not sold under a brand name. Teva has also begun creating its own drugs. Its biggest seller is Copaxone, which is used to treat Parkinson's disease.

FROM FARMS TO FACTORIES

For the Medical Minded

Teens who hope to enter the medical profession can start their training while still in high school by volunteering for the Magen David Adom (MDA), which serves as Israel's Red Cross. Teens as young as 13 can begin learning skills, and at 15 they can ride on ambulances sent to medical emergencies. The teens of MDA learn paramedic skills and treat the wounded during natural disasters or terrorist attacks. Yulia Tskahy, 17, told a reporter in 2006 that some of her friends think she's crazy for volunteering for the MDA. But she hopes to be a doctor and added, "I want to be useful…. I don't want to sit home … watching TV."

Yulia Tskahy is a fully-trained medic at 17.

Mount Meron, Israel's highest point, is a popular place to hike.

6

Serious About Fun

THE THREAT OF WAR AND VIOLENCE HANGS OVER MUCH OF ISRAELI LIFE. But the country's teens are hardly filled with gloom and doom. To escape the pressures of their special situation—and the stress of everyday life—Israelis find pleasure in as many ways as they can. Israeli teens travel with their friends and families to vacation spots, where they can take part in active pastimes, such as hiking or swimming. Visiting historical sites helps keep them in touch with their people's past.

Israeli teens also enjoy movies, television shows, and popular music of all kinds. And they join clubs, pursue hobbies, hang out at malls with their friends, and play and watch sports.

Israel
Topographical
Map

LEBANON

Hurshat Tal
National Park

Mt. Meron

Hills of Galilee

SYRIA

Golan
Hts.

Golan
Heights

Sea of
Galilee

Haifa

Jezreel
Valley

JORDAN

Tel Aviv-
Yafo

West
Bank

Jordan River

Mediterranean
Sea

Jerusalem

Gaza
Strip

Dead
Sea

Masada
National
Park

Negev
Desert

JORDAN

N
W E
S

0   20   40 mi.
0   20   40 km

EGYPT

Eliat

Red
Sea

The Great Outdoors

Israel is a small country, just over 8,000 square miles (20,800 square km). But within its borders, Israel offers its citizens and tourists a wide range of things to see and do. Along the Mediterranean, beautiful beaches attract teens wanting to swim, play in the sand, or merely bake in the sun. A tiny corner of southern Israel borders the Red Sea, and there the town of Eliat attracts visitors looking for fun in the sun. Eliat has been called Israel's "First City," since it was the Jews' first stop in Israel after they left their slavery in Egypt thousands of years ago. Water sports such as snorkeling, surfing, windsurfing, sailing, and water-skiing are popular pastimes for teens at the seashore in Eliat and at beaches along the Mediterranean.

For a restful day near water without a trip to the beach, Israelis head to the Dead Sea. The high level of salt in its waters makes it easy for people to float on the surface.

Soothing Mud

Playing in mud can get some kids in trouble. But Israeli teens are encouraged to sit in the mud from the Dead Sea. The mud contains the same healthful salt and minerals found in the Dead Sea's waters. Visitors to the Dead Sea, young and old, enjoy sitting in "baths" of Dead Sea mud.

The mud is said to take poisons out of the body and keep skin feeling soft. Heated mud is also used as part of a treatment for some physical problems, such as arthritis. Mud from the Dead Sea is packaged and sold around the world as a beauty treatment.

Covering one's self with mud and posing for a photo with friends is considered a rite of passage.

The Dead Sea's shore is more than 1,300 feet (396 meters) below sea level, making it the lowest spot of land on Earth. The sea is slowly drying up, because the river that flows into it, the Jordan, is increasingly used for irrigation. But it will take thousands of years before this huge sea disappears.

Mini Israel

Teens who want to see all of Israel's tourist spots in one day come to Mini Israel, a park between Jerusalem and Tel Aviv. On 13 acres (5.3 hectares) of land, model builders—most of them Russian immigrants—have created small, detailed models of Israel's natural wonders and famous buildings. Visitors can tower above a model of Jerusalem, see snow-topped Mount Meron, and admire the beaches and skyscrapers of Tel Aviv. Mini Israel has about 350 models, including a Biblical Zoo, with the animals Noah brought with him on the ark. The park is also a source of jobs for some teens, who work in Mini Israel's restaurants and snack stands.

Near the Dead Sea is Israel's most popular national park, Masada. Its rocky cliffs tower over the nearby countryside. On the top is an ancient fort, where Jewish rebels launched a rebellion against the Roman Empire almost 2,000 years ago. Jewish teens from Israel and around the world come to the fort to see first-hand an important part of Israel's history.

The second most popular park in Israel is farther north, in a region called Galilee. Hurshat Tal Nature Reserve draws families seeking to camp, fish, swim, and barbecue. Teens and younger kids especially like to splash down the park's waterslides, which are some of the highest in the country.

Not all Israelis go back to nature on their travels. Some head to the important religious sites in Jerusalem. The city

Inside the Church of the Holy Sepulchre, a structure called an edicule holds what some experts believe is the tomb where Jesus Christ was buried.

SERIOUS ABOUT FUN

has sites holy to Jews, Christians, and Muslims. For Jews, the Western Wall is the most important religious site in the world. The wall is all that remains of the Second Temple, which the Romans destroyed in the first century A.D. Today Jews of all ages come to pray at the wall.

For Christians, Jerusalem has the sites that Jesus Christ visited before his death. It also has the Church of the Holy Sepulchre, which dates to the 12th century, though a church from the fourth century also once sat on the spot. The churches were built at the place where Jesus was thought to have been nailed to a cross. Israeli Muslims come to Jerusalem to see the Dome of the Rock. Muslims believe Muhammad rose into heaven from the spot where the shrine stands.

Film star Yehuda Levi attended a high school that was focused on the arts.

Leisure Time at Home

Israeli teens and their families don't have to travel far to be entertained or have a good time. High-tech gadgets keep teens from being bored at home. They can play the latest video games, watch DVDs, cable or satellite TV, and download songs onto their MP3 players. Television shows include programs from Europe and the United States as well as Israeli shows. Popular local shows in 2006 included *Yaztpan*, a late-night talk show hosted by comedian Eli Yaztpan, and *Mis'hak Mahur* (*Fixed Game*), a show featuring comics commenting on current events. Israel also has its own film industry, and one popular young star is Yehuda Levi, known for his good looks.

Young Israelis listen to songs in many of the musical styles popular

with teens across the world, especially rock, pop, and hip-hop. In recent years, U.S. artists, such as the Black Eyed Peas and 50 Cent, were popular performance acts in Israel. Young Israeli musicians adopt American musical styles and write their songs in Hebrew. Such groups as Hadag Nahash and Subliminal feature hip-hop.

One of the biggest Israeli stars is Sarit Hadad, who has been called Israel's Madonna. Most of her records have gone triple-platinum, meaning they have sold more than 120,000 copies in Israel—a large number for such a small country. Aviv Geffen is a rock musician popular in Europe as well as Israel. His father was a folk singer, and Aviv writes songs that call for peace between Israelis and Palestinians. Other singers blend musical styles from the Middle East with hip-hop and rock. Israeli Arabs record music that blends various musical styles while singing in Arabic.

American and European cultures also influence what Israeli teens read. Popular books are translated into Hebrew, while many people read them in their original language. Some popular, classic English-language authors include Roald Dahl, Ernest Hemingway, and C.S. Lewis. A number of Israeli authors have risen to international fame. Most, such as Orly Castel-Bloom, Amos Oz, and A.B. Yahoshua write in Hebrew. Another popular Israeli writer is David Grossman, who

Favorite books by David Grossman include The Zigzag Kid and Duel.

Reading Russian

The large number of Russian immigrants in Israel has led some companies to publish newspapers in Russian. The largest is called *Vesti*, and in the early 2000s, it published a special section for teens called "Teenager Plus." In it, Russian teens shared some of their thoughts on life in Israel and relations with *tsabarim*, kids born in Israel. One Russian wrote, "We have different interests, read different books, and listen to different music."

tsabarim
TSAH-bahr-im

has also written for teens and children. The many books of Levin Kipnis, a prize-winning writer who died in 1990, are still popular with children. Almost everyone in Israel can read, and magazines and newspapers are popular reading material for most adults.

Staying Active

Like teens the world over, Israelis enjoy playing and watching a variety of sports. Across the country, hundreds of thousands of people take part in sports such as football (soccer), basketball, swimming, volleyball, tennis, gymnastics, and martial arts.

Jewish immigrants from around the world have brought the sports of their native lands to Israel. They play such sports as cricket, softball, and lawn bowling, and a few Frisbee teams have formed. For younger children and teens, organized leagues for team sports are run by schools and community groups. The most talented young athletes attend the Wingate Institute of Physical Education and Sports near Netanya, where they receive special training in their chosen sport. Athletes from around the world train at the institute, and it is a leader in the study of sports medicine.

Israeli teens of all backgrounds are active in sports.

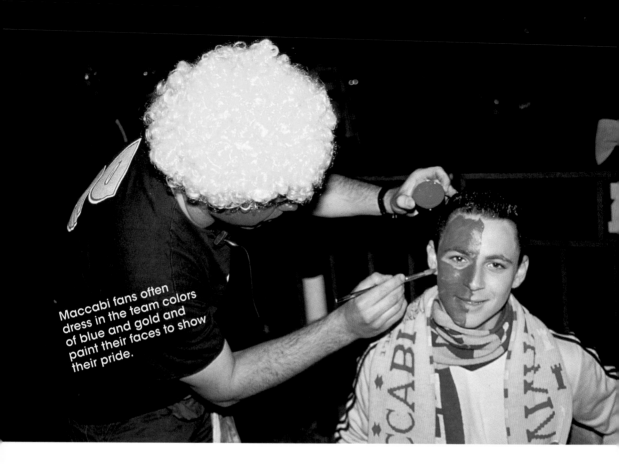

Maccabi fans often dress in the team colors of blue and gold and paint their faces to show their pride.

The most popular spectator sports are basketball and football (soccer). Tel Aviv's Maccabi basketball team is the most popular professional team in any sport, and it has won several European championships.

Israel's national football team competes in the World Cup, and players such as Eyal Berkovic and Tal Ben-Haim are Israeli football heroes who have gone on to have great professional careers in Europe. Adam Argeband, an aspiring teen football player, said Ben-Haim is "living the dream of every young Israeli footballer."

Every four years, Jewish athletes from Israel and around the world gather for the Maccabiah Games. Similar to the Olympics, the games feature events in more than 30 sports, including track and field, swimming and diving, and judo. In 2005, around 7,000 athletes from 55 countries took part in the games. At those games, 18-year-old Shane Solomon, a South African table-tennis player noted, "The standard [of competition] was very high."

Olympic Honor

Israel has sent athletes to the Summer Olympics since 1952. Its first gold medal, however, did not come until the 2004 games in Athens.

Gal Fridman took home a gold in windsurfing. When he received his medal, he paid tribute to 11 Israeli athletes killed by Palestinian terrorists at the 1972 Munich games. The attack on the Israeli athletes shocked the world, and it was the subject of the 2005 movie *Munich*. Fridman said, "We think about them [the 11 athletes] all the time. They're always in our mind. When I get home, I will go to the memorial place for them and show them the gold medal."

Gal Fridman began windsurfing at age 6.

Israel's scouts participate in public events such as parades.

Youth Movements & Clubs

For Israeli teens who don't want to play team sports, joining a youth movement is another way to get together with other kids. Even before Israel was founded, Jewish political groups in Europe formed such clubs for teens. Their goal was to teach the youth about Zionism, the effort of Jews to regain their biblical homeland. Members of these youth movements began settling in Palestine, and they helped spark the interest in kibbutzim. Other youth movements, such as Jerusalem's Beni Akiva, were dedicated to Orthodox religious teachings as well as Zionism.

Today Israel has one national youth movement, the Tzofim, or Scouts. The organization was founded in 1919 as a Zionist youth movement. Both boys and girls belong to the same groups. The Tzofim include Jews and Arabs and both secular and religious teens. It has a total membership of about 85,000. Members do volunteer work, camp, and hike outdoors.

Some of the older youth movements tied to political and religious groups still exist. The Zionist groups have often split along political lines, with each national party sponsoring its own group. Membership numbers for most groups are falling. Because Israel is now a more established nation, the appeal of Zionism is not as strong. More Israeli youth seem to want to focus on their own goals during their school years.

The Tzofim Oath & Commandments

In eighth grade, all Israeli Scouts take the following oath: "I promise to do my best to fulfill my duties to my people, my country and my land, to help others at all times, and to obey the Scouts law." The Scouts also live by these commandments:

The Scout is trustworthy.
The Scout is loyal to his people, his country and his language.
The Scout is a useful member of the society, loves work, and helps others.
The Scout is friend to everyone, and brother to all scouts.
The Scout is polite.
The Scout loves nature and protects it.
The Scout is obedient.
The Scout never loses hope.
The Scout is thrifty.
The Scout is pure in his speech and deeds.

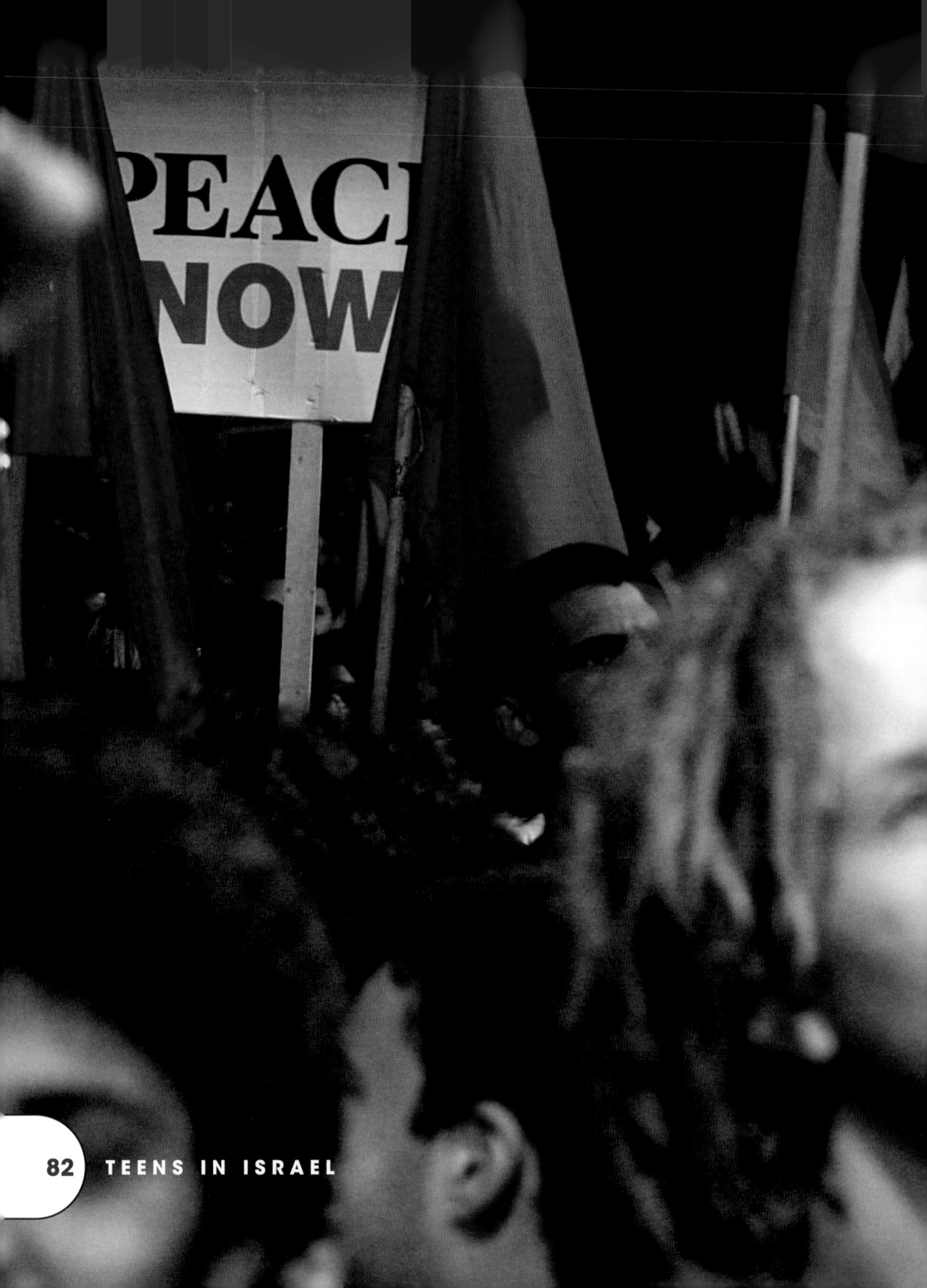
PEAC
NOW

Looking Ahead

ANCIENT WALLS AND GLEAMING GLASS BUILDINGS. Desert heat and mountain snows. Arabs, Jews, and Druze. Muslims, Christians, and haredim. From almost any angle, it's easy to see that the tiny nation of Israel is filled with variety. But no one forgets that Israel is a Jewish nation founded so the Jews would have a homeland. Most of them have one thing in common: a sense of shared history and culture. That culture, though, can be expressed in different ways.

The teens of Israel know about their shared past, but knowing the future is impossible. Despite its wealth from high technology, Israel has a growing gap between its richest citizens and its poorest. Conditions tend to be worse for the non-Jews and the ultra-Orthodox. And Israel faces threats from abroad, because some Arabs claim Israel does not have a right to exist.

Young Jewish and Arab Israelis may hold the key to the future of Israel. Their ability to get along may determine whether Israel has lasting peace or constantly faces the threat of war.

At a Glance

Official name: State of Israel

Capital: Jerusalem

People

Population: 6,352,117

Population by age group:
0-14 years: 26.3%
15-64 years: 63.9%
65 years and over: 9.8%

Life expectancy at birth: 79.46 years

Official languages: Hebrew and Arabic

Other languages: English and Russian

Religion:
Jewish: 76.4%
Muslim: 16%
Christian: 2.1%
Druze: 1.6%
Unspecified: 3.9%

Legal ages
Alcohol consumption: 18
Driver's license: 17 with a parent, 17½ without
Employment: 15
Leave school: 15
Marriage: 17, though exceptions are made
Military service: 18
Voting: 18

Government

Type of government: Parliamentary democracy

Chief of state: President, elected by the lawmaking body

Head of government: Prime minister, elected by popular vote

Lawmaking body: Knesset, elected by popular vote

Administrative divisions: Six districts

Independence: May 14, 1948 (from League of Nations mandate under British administration)

National symbols: A six-sided star called the Magen David, named for Israel's first king. The country's official emblem features a menorah, a candlestick that holds seven candles.

Geography

Total Area: 8,308 square miles (20,770 square kilometers)

Climate: Temperate to tropical; hot and dry in southern and eastern areas; rainy season from November through April; dry from May to October; heaviest rainfall in the north and center.

Highest point: Mount Meron 3,986 feet (1,208 meters)

Lowest point: Dead Sea, 1,346 feet (408 meters) below sea level

Major river: Jordan

Major landforms: Coastal plain along the Mediterranean Sea, Golan Heights, the hills of Galilee, Jezreel Valley, the Negev Desert

Economy

Currency: New Israeli Shekel

Population below poverty line: 21%

Major natural resources: Copper ore, food products, gravel and stone, sand, clay, limestone, gypsum, potash, bromine, magnesium, salt, phosphates

Major agricultural products: Citrus, vegetables, cotton, beef, poultry, dairy products

Major exports: Polished diamonds, chemicals and chemical products, electronics, machinery, transportation equipment, clothing, flowers, fruits, vegetables

Major imports: Rough diamonds, machinery, fuels, raw materials, grains, consumer goods

Historical Timeline

Israel's King Solomon builds the first temple on a site chosen by his father, David

 British colonies are established in North America

Triggered by a revolution in Russia, the Third Aliyah (1919–1923) begins; eventually 40,000 Jews from Eastern Europe arrive

Period of outside rule begins as Greeks take control of Israel; Roman and Byzantine empires later rule the region; the Romans call Israel and the surrounding area Palestine

Government-sanctioned violence against Jews leads thousands of Russian Jews to go to Palestine in the Second Aliyah (1904–1914)

Ancestors of modern Jews settle in what is now Israel

c. 2000 B.C.	960 B.C	776 B.C.	332 B.C.	636	1517	1600s	1882	1904	1919

First recorded Olympic Games

Arab Muslims take control of the Middle East

First arrival of a large number of European Jewish immigrants in Palestine in what is known as the First Aliyah (1882–1903)

Turkish Ottoman Empire rules Palestine until 1917 when driven out by the British during World War I (1914–1918)

 Bronze Age well established in Europe

 Historical World Event

The Fifth Aliyah (1929–1939)
begins as Nazis come to power
in Germany; 250,000 Jews,
mainly from Germany and
Eastern Europe, arrive by 1940

Palestinian terrorists kill
11 Israeli athletes at
the Summer Olympics
in Munich, Germany

 During World War II,
Nazi Germany carries
out the Holocaust,
the murder of 6
million Jews

The Six-Day War is fought
between Israel and its Arab
neighbors; Israel captures
the Sinai Peninsula, Golan
Heights, East Jerusalem, and
the West Bank

1924   1929   1939–1945   1948   1949   1967   1969   1972

The state of Israel is created;
hundreds of thousands of Arab
Palestinians leave the country

 The U.S. stock market
crashes, and severe
worldwide economic
depression sets in

 Two U.S.
astronauts land
on the moon

The Fourth Aliyah (1924–1929)
begins; 82,000 Jews, mainly
from Poland and Hungary,
arrive by 1929

Operation Magic Carpet
begins; the mission
brings 49,000 Jews
out of Yemen to
Israel; a similar
operation follows
in 1951 to bring
Jews out of Iraq

Historical Timeline

Hamas, a terrorist and political organization, gains control of the Palestinian Authority, increasing fears in Israel of more violence; war breaks out between Israel and Hezbollah, a terrorist organization based in Lebanon

At a meeting with U.S. President Jimmy Carter, Israeli Prime Minister Menachem Begin and Egyptian President Anwar Sadat sign a peace treaty; a peace agreement with Jordan follows in 1994, ending 46 years of war

 Soviet Union collapses

Palestinians in Gaza and the West Bank begin the First Intifada, a violent uprising against Israeli rule; the Second Intifada follows in 2000

Israel removes Jewish settlers and soldiers from Gaza.

1973	1978	1984	1987	1989	1991	1993	2001	2005	2006

A secret mission called Operation Moses brings 8,000 Ethiopian Jews to Israel; Operation Solomon in 1991 brings 14,000 more

Israel agrees to give Palestinians self-rule in Gaza and Jericho, part of the West Bank.

Egypt and Syria launch a surprise attack in the Yom Kippur War; after initial losses, Israel defeats the invaders

 The Berlin Wall falls

Terrorist attacks on the two World Trade Center Towers in New York City and on the Pentagon in Washington, D.C., leave thousands dead

Glossary

binational	having people from two nationalities or ethnic groups
covenant	a formal and permanent agreement
Diaspora	the scattering of a group of people from their homeland to many nations; usually capitalized when referring to the Jews; it also refers to the lands where they settled
electives	courses that students can choose to take but are not required
extracurricular	referring to activities that occur outside a school's normal classes
nomads	people who wander from place to place to make a living, often as shepherds
Orthodox	a strict form of Judaism that calls for closely following the teachings in the Torah
prejudice	hatred or unfair treatment of people who belong to a certain social group, such as a race or religion
Sabbath	the day of the week that is designated for rest and religious services
secular	not religious; trusting science and knowledge over faith in God
vocational schools	schools that prepare students to enter a particular field of employment, usually a field that requires skilled workers, such as mechanics, plumbers, or carpenters

Additional Resources

IN THE LIBRARY

Carew-Miller, Anna. *The Palestinians.*
Philadelphia: Mason Crest
Publishers, 2004.

Goldstein, Margaret J. *Israel in Pictures.*
Minneapolis: Lerner Publications,
2004.

Greenfeld, Howard. *A Promise Fulfilled:
Theodor Hertzl, Chaim Weitzmann,
and David Ben-Gurion, and the
Creation of the State of Israel.* New
York: Greenwillow Books, 2005.

Hintz, Martin. *Israel.* Rev. ed. New York:
Children's Press, 2006.

Keene, Michael. *Judaism.* Milwaukee:
World Almanac Library, 2006.

Minnis, Ivan. *The Arab-Israeli Conflict.*
Austin: Raintree Steck-Vaughn, 2003.

Roy, Jennifer. *Israel.* New York:
Benchmark Books, 2004.

ON THE WEB

For more information on this topic, use
FactHound.
1. Go to *www.facthound.com*
2. Type in this book ID: 0756524431
3. Click on the *Fetch It* button.

Look for more Global Connections books.

Teens in Australia
Teens in Brazil
Teens in China
Teens in France
Teens in India
Teens in Japan
Teens in Kenya

Teens in Mexico
Teens in Russia
Teens in Saudi Arabia
Teens in Spain
Teens in Venezuela
Teens in Vietnam

Source Notes

Page 17, line 27: Dina Kraft. "Quiet Crisis." *The Jewish Week* 11 Jan. 2006. 4 Oct. 2006. www.thejewishweek.com/bottom/specialcontent.php3?artid=1079&print=yes

Page 17, line 34: Ibid.

Page 18, column 2, line 14: Adam Argeband. E-mail interview. 22 May 2006.

Page 27, column 1, line 1: Ada Ushpiz. "Doves Among the Druze." *Haaretz* 8 March 2004. 27 April 2006. www.haaretz.com/hasen/objects/pages/PrintArticleEn.jhtml?itemNo=401368

Page 28, sidebar, line 25: Talia Carman. "The Circassians of Rihania." *Circassian World* May 2001. 28 April 2006. www.circassianworld.com/Israel.html

Page 29, sidebar, line 12: Donna Rosenthal. *The Israelis: Ordinary People in an Extraordinary Land.* New York: Free Press, 2003, p. 248.

Page 30, column 2, line 13: Ibid., p. 104.

Page 32, column 1, line 11: "Civil Disobedience on the Rise Among Jewish Teens." *WorldTribune.com.* 2 Feb. 2006. 4 Oct. 2006. www.worldtribune.com/worldtribune/WTARC/2006/me_israel_02_02.html

Page 32, column 1, line 17: Orr Redko. E-mail interview. 24 May 2006.

Page 33, column 1, line 14: Joan Nathan. *The Foods of Israel Today.* New York: Alfred A. Knopf, 2001, p. 62.

Page 40, column 2, line 6: Ruth Katz. "Expectations of Family Life in a Multicultural Context: An Israeli Example." *International Journal of Sociology of the Family* Vol. 30 No. 1 (Fall 2002). 4 Oct. 2006. www.yorku.ca/irjs/Archives/F20/F201.pdf

Page 42, line 10: Micaela Terk. E-mail interview. 22 May 2006.

Page 43, column 1, line 15: *The Israelis: Ordinary People in an Extraordinary Land*, p. 175.

Page 43, column 2, line 4: Amira Feldman. E-mail interview. 23 May 2006.

Page 45, column 2, line 5: "What People Say About Peace Child Israel." Peace Child Israel. 21 Nov. 2006. www.mideastweb.org/peacechild/testimonials.html

Page 53, column 1, line 8: Michael Kozakov. E-mail interview. 23 May 2006.

Page 60, column 1, line 25: Ben Argeband. E-mail interview. 22 May 2006.

Page 62, column 1, line 3: *The Israelis: Ordinary People in an Extraordinary Land*, p. 47.

Page 63, column 1, line 1: Ronen Tal. "Youth Volunteers: Does Anyone Care?" *Ynet News.com* 19 Dec. 2005. 4 Oct. 2006. www.ynetnews.com/articles/0,7340,L-3186968,00.html

Page 63, column 1, line 13: "Shinshin Volunteers Present a Face for Israel." Jewish Agency for Israel Volume 9, Issue 4 (April 2006). 4 Oct. 2006. http://194.90.65.227/JewishAgency/English/Home/Jewish+Agency+Resources/Personal+Stories/Archive/2006/aprilb06.htm

Page 63, column 2, line 6: "Eyal Brami Update." American Friends Service Committee 5 May 2006. www.afsc.org/israel-palestine/activism/eyal-update.htm

Page 69, column 2, line 7: Jennie Matthew, "Israeli Teens Bolster Emergency Frontlines." *The Manilla Times*. 14 Sept. 2006. 21 Nov. 2006. www.manilatimes.net/national/2006/sept/14/yehey/opinion/20060914opi6.html

Page 76, sidebar, line 11: *The Israelis: Ordinary People in an Extraordinary Land*, p. 145.

Page 78, column 1, line 14: Adam Argeband. E-mail interview. 22 May 2006.

Page 78, column 2, line 13: Joel Leyden. "Israel Maccabiah Sports Games Bring Smiles To Jewish Nation." *Israel News Agency* 21 July 2005. 4 Oct. 2006. www.israelnewsagency.com/israelmaccabiah480722.html

Page 79, column 2, line 8: Arthur Spiegelman. "Israeli Surfs in for Historic Gold." *Washington Times* 26 August 2004. 5 Oct. 2006. www.washingtontimes.com/national/20040826-122103-2394r.htm

Pages 84–85, At a Glance: United States. Central Intellegence Agency. *The World Factbook—Israel*. 17 Oct. 2006. 30 Oct. 2006. www.cia.gov/cia/publications/factbook/geos/is.html

Select Bibliography

Avi-Yohan, Michael, ed. *A History of Israel and the Holy Land.* Continuum Publishing Group, 2001.

Bell, Brian, and Simon Griver, eds. *Insight Guides: Israel.* Fifth ed. Long Island City, N.Y.: Langenscheidt Publishers, 2006.

Dowty, Alan, ed. *Critical Issues in Israeli Society.* Westport, Conn.: Praeger Publishers, 2004.

Dowty, Alan. *Israel/Palestine.* Malden, Mass.: Polity Press, 2005.

Kadish, Joanna. "Ethiopian Jewish Journalist Visits Seattle from Israel to Share His Story." Jewish Federation of Greater Seattle. 5 Oct. 2006. www.jewishinseattle. org/JF/Giving/Annual/Ethiopian_Jewish_journalist.doc

Katz, Ruth. "Expectations of Family Life in a Multicultural Context: An Israeli Example." *International Journal of Sociology of the Family* Vol. 30 No. 1 (Fall 2002). 7 Sept. 2006. www.yorku.ca/irjs/Archives/F20/F201.pdf

Kraft, Dina. "Quiet Crisis." *The Jewish Week* 11 Jan. 2006. 4 Oct. 2006. www.thejewishweek.com/bottom/specialcontent. php3?artid=1079&print=yes

Leyden, Joel. "Israel Maccabiah Sports Games Bring Smiles To Jewish Nation." *Israel News Agency* 21 July 2005. 7 Sept. 2006. www. israelnewsagency.com/israelmaccabiah480722.html

Migdal, Joel S. *Through the Lens of Israel: Explorations in State and Society.* Albany: State University Press of New York, 2001.

Nathan, Joan. *The Foods of Israel Today.* New York: Alfred A. Knopf, 2001.

Rosenthal, Donna. *The Israelis: Ordinary People in an Extraordinary Land.* New York: Free Press, 2003.

"Roundtable: Education Reform in Israel." *Yale Israel Journal* 8 (Winter 2006). 1 Aug. 2006. www.yaleisraeljournal.com/ wintr2006/roundtable.php

Index

About the Author
Michael Burgan

Michael Burgan is a freelance writer of books for children and adults. A history graduate of the University of Connecticut, he has written more than 100 fiction and nonfiction children's books. For adult audiences, he has written news articles, essays, and plays. Michael is a recipient of an Educational Press Association of America award.

About the Content Adviser
Karen Grumberg, Ph.D.

Our content adviser for *Teens in Israel*, Karen Grumberg, is an assistant professor in the Department of Middle Eastern Studies at the University of Texas at Austin. Her main research interests are contemporary Hebrew literature and Jewish-American literature.

Image Credits

David Silverman/Getty Images, cover, 17 (bottom), 34, 60, 63; Kobby Dagen/BigStockPhoto, back cover (top); Nola Rin/Shutterstock, back cover (bottom), 1 (left); Israelimages/Israel Talby, 1 (middle left), 10, 15, 18, 27, 31, 33 (top), 35 (all), 40, 44, 61, 64–65; Eyal Ofer/Corbis, 1 (middle right), 24; NEO/Shutterstock, 1 (right); Darrell J. Rohl/Shutterstock, 2–3; Alex Slobodkin/iStockphoto, 4; Lior Filshteiner/Shutterstock, 5; Dario Diament/BigStockPhoto, 7 (top); Corel, 7 (middle); Ron Zafrir/iStockphoto, 7 (bottom left); Odelia Cohen/Shutterstock, 7 (bottom right), 58; Israelimages/Win Robins, 8; Israelimages/Hashomer Hatzair, 13; Uriel Sinai/Getty Images, 16–17; Salem Suhaib/Reuters/Corbis, 19; Israelimages/Elyssa Frank, 20; Israelimages/Naftali Hilger, 23; Eyalos/Shutterstock, 25; Paula Bronstein/Getty Images, 26; Israelimages/Yasha Mazur, 28–29, 39; Israelimages/Hanan Isachar, 30, 51, 53; Alaa Badarneh/epa/Corbis, 32 (top); Israelimages/Richard Nowitz, 32–33, 49; Shaul Schwarz/Getty Images, 36; Israelimages/Aliza Auerbach, 38; Israelimages/Karen Benzian, 41; Israelimages/Michael Levit, 42–43; Courtesy Peace Child Israel, 45; Israelimages/Iral Teitelbaum, 46, 56–57; Israelimages/Iral Tal, 50; Israelimages/Garo Nalbandian, 54; Brian Hendler/Getty Images, 55; Israelimages/Yuval Gilad, 62; Paul A. Souders/Corbis, 67; Jack Guez/AFP/Getty Images, 69; Israelimages/Ruthie Talby, 70; Barbara Davidson/Dallas Morning News/Corbis, 73; Sandro Vannini/Corbis, 74–75; Yossi Zwecker, 75 (top); Israelimages/Dan Porges, 76; Israelimages/Steven Allan, 77; Israelimages/Hezi Asher, 78; Clive Mason/Getty Images, 79; Hanan Isachar/Corbis, 80; Yonathan Weitzman/Corbis, 82; Nancy Olson/BigStockPhoto, 84 (top); Mary Lane/Shutterstock, 84 (bottom); Photodisc, 85 (top); Bryan Firestone/Shutterstock, 85 (bottom); Igor Shootov/BigStockPhoto, 90.